STATE AID
AND EDUCATIONAL
OPPORTUNITY

STATE AID
AND EDUCATIONAL
OPPORTUNITY

GAIL R. WILENSKY

*Published with cooperation from the Institute for Public Policy Research,
University of Michigan*

with a Foreword by JOHN P. CRECINE, Director

 SAGE PUBLICATIONS, Beverly Hills, California

For information address:

Sage Publications, Inc.
275 South Beverly Drive
Beverly Hills, California 90212

Printed in the United States of America

Library of Congress Catalog Card No. 73-92357

Standard Book Number: 8039-0064-3

First Printing

CONTENTS

TABLES

FIGURES

FOREWORD

This study is the outgrowth of research conducted by Dr. Wilensky while a research assistant in the Institute of Public Policy Studies (then, the Institute of Public Administration) at the University of Michigan. It is the kind of policy-oriented research which we as an institution encourage: research which, in addition to generating knowledge with more immediate social utility, uses real-world concerns and applications to raise questions with important consequences for basic theory. We see a close and mutually beneficial relationship between basic and applied social science research with real situations and problems directing the scholar's attention to important and relevant extensions of theory. This study also reflects the belief that the concerns of normative theory (how the world ought to be) are most likely to be useful when consciously related to positive theory (descriptions of the way the world *is* and why).

The questions addressed in this book, although specifically applied to elementary and secondary education, have general applicability to the class of public programs financed at one level of government, but actually carried out by a lower level of government. The issue raised also apply to any funding agency, public or private, attempting to effect a change in institutional or individual behavior by providing earmarked funds. Does a grant of money earmarked for a particular program or purpose merely substitute for funds that would have otherwise been provided for the program through other sources or does the grant represent a net addition of resources for the program? Even if the grant does result in higher levels of spending for a given function (education), do more dollars make a corresponding difference in the quality of the function or its output? Will the same formula for distributing grants work in the same way for different recipients? These are all important questions for public policy and for policy makers.

As we see trends toward the decentralization of governmental operations and a corresponding centralization of revenue sources, it is clear that the formulae and procedures used by central authorities to distribute resources among decentralized units take on added importance. What are these procedures designed to accomplish (e.g., equalize educational opportunities, etc.); are they in fact doing what they set out to do? These are all issues addressed in the context of educational programs in this volume; the implications of this study for other issues of current interest such as revenue sharing, decentralization of HUD regional offices, Model Cities programs, other federal grant-in-aid programs, weight-and-gas tax rebates to local governments for street repairs, community action programs, etc., are obvious.

This is the type of analysis which, ideally, should be undertaken before a government funding program is adopted and, perhaps in a less rigorous form, by the makers of public policy rather than by academics. We hope that studies like this will serve as appropriate models for public officials and students of public policy and administration.

Dr. Wilensky's work has raised our Institute's benefit/ cost ratio for 1967-68 significantly; not only where benefit is measured in terms of research output—but in terms of the quality of purely human, social interactions, as well.

John Patrick Crecine, *Director*
Institute of Public Policy Studies
The University of Michigan

Ann Arbor, Michigan
January, 1970

ACKNOWLEDGMENTS

In writing this study, I have received helpful comments from many people. Some of these individuals are mentioned below. To the rest, I express a collective "thank you."

I am grateful to the Institute of Public Policy Studies at the University of Michigan for providing financial assistance and a congenial working atmosphere, both of which facilitated the writing of this study.

Three associates have been particularly helpful. I wish to thank Bruce Gensemer for making available much of the data he had collected for his own work, and Gunter Schramm and Emil Sunley for having read the entire original manuscript and having made many helpful suggestions.

I also wish to thank W. H. Locke Anderson, Robin Barlow, Harvey E. Brazer, and Robert S. Friedman, who have made many valuable comments and suggestions, for which I am grateful.

I am especially indebted to Professor Brazer for the encouragement and interest he has shown during the past several years. He has been responsible for sparking much of my interest in public finance and has deeply influenced my thinking and understanding of economic issues.

Finally, I wish to express thanks to my husband, Robert. Without his patience and encouragement, this study would have been impossible.

INTRODUCTION

The role of intergovernmental grants in the financing of local expenditures recently has become a prominent area of concern among economists, policy makers, and public-minded citizens. This study is concerned with one of the earliest of such grants—state aid to primary and secondary education. Its focal point is the effect of the current state aid program in Michigan.

The evaluation of the Michigan program proceeds on two levels. First, the Michigan program is evaluated as a foundation program, with both the structural framework and the objectives of the foundation program accepted as given. Second, the foundation program itself is evaluated as a method of distributing state aid. This portion of the study is relevant to almost all programs of state aid to education rather than only to Michigan's, since almost all states base their programs of aid on the concept of a foundation program. Prior to the evaluation of the foundation program itself, attention is focused on the effects of state aid on the local district's expenditure decisions. For this portion of the analysis, we rely on basic demand theory. Proceeding in this manner not only enables us to evaluate the foundation program but also provides a basis for formulating alternative programs of aid.

This study is therefore both "positive" and "normative" in nature. It is positive in so far as it is concerned with the way the existing program operates. It is normative in so far as it is concerned with the way the program "should" operate. The normative issues are first viewed relative to the general framework provided by economic theory, and then according to several implicit or explicitly stated social objectives, including the stated objectives of the existing program itself.

In Chapter 1, a general economic framework of grants for education is developed, based on considerations of efficiency and interpersonal income redistribution.

Chapter 2 considers the expressed objectives of the state aid program and the implications of these objectives.

Chapter 3 provides a description of the current program, an analysis of some of the recent changes in the program in terms of the distribution of state funds, and an evaluation of the Michigan program as a foundation program.

Chapter 4 considers alternative foundation programs and compares the resulting distribution with the distribution of state funds under the current program.

Chapter 5 is concerned with the effects of state aid on the local district's expenditure decisions. Its purposes are to develop a theoretical analysis of districts' reactions to various types of grants and to estimate the effects of the current program.

Chapter 6 is concerned with the policy implications of the theoretical analysis of Chapter 5, given the general framework and expressed objectives developed in Chapters 1 and 2.

The main conclusions of the study are:

(1) The evaluation of the Michigan program in terms of its own objectives implies evaluating the program as a foundation program. The major objective of the foundation program is to equalize educational opportunity. This is interpreted to mean the avoidance of unacceptable differences in the availability of educational services. Within the framework of the foundation program, the Michigan program is defi-

cient. A secondary objective of the Michigan program is to increase the level of educational services in general. Assuming a direct relationship between expenditures on education and quality of educational services, the purpose of the grant is to increase the district's educational expenditures.

(2) The standard foundation program is composed of a required local contribution and a unit or lump-sum grant from the state. Under the foundation program, state aid is distributed either as a lump-sum grant or as a "stimulative minimum" grant. Which, depends on whether the required contribution is less or greater than what would otherwise be spent.

(3) Both types of grants are objectionable. The lump-sum grant is inefficient. It only affects the resources available to the district; it does not provide any encouragement for expenditures on education as opposed to expenditures on anything else. The stimulative minimum grant is efficient but is likely to be ineffective because some districts may not participate.

(4) The structure of the foundation program is inappropriate to its own objectives. Thus the fundamental criticism of the Michigan program is not that it is deficient as a foundation program but that it *is* a foundation program.

(5) A matching grant, where the matching begins at a level which is greater than zero and less than an estimate of the district's would-be expenditures, is an efficient way of increasing the district's expenditures on education. It can therefore be used to accomplish the major objectives of state aid to education.

A GENERAL FRAMEWORK FOR GRANTS TO EDUCATION

From the standpoint of economic theory, two aspects of the state aid program are of concern. The first involves allocative efficiency: the use of intergovernmental grants to compensate for benefit (and/or cost) spillovers. The second involves interpersonal income distribution: the use of expenditures on education as a means of redistributing income among the present and the future generation.

ALLOCATIVE EFFICIENCY

The discussion of allocative efficiency assumes an economy similar to our own—that is, an economy based on consumer sovereignty and one in which reliance on the pricing mechanism of the market can be expected, in most cases, to result in an optimum (efficient) allocation of resources.[1] One of the assumptions underlying reliance on a market system to achieve an efficient allocation is that individuals act as though they allocate their resources so that marginal benefits are equal to marginal costs across all goods. The problem is that there is a variety of goods, which results in a spillover of benefits (or costs) to persons other than the one directly consuming the good. Because the individual will take into account only the benefits which accrue to himself, reliance on the market mechanism for goods involving spillovers results in a nonoptimal allocation of resources.[2]

The objective of this section is limited to enumerating the likely spillovers.[3] Brief consideration is given to some suggestive evidence regarding spillovers from education and also to some of the major complications associated with the quantification of these spillovers. At the end of the section some suggestions are offered regarding the nature of an intergovernmental grant which appears to be implied in view of the spillovers.

Benefit Theory

An ideal system for the financing of goods with substantial spillovers is provided by the subjective benefit (or voluntary exchange) theory of taxation. Under the benefit approach, taxes serve as proxies for prices, and individuals are taxed in accordance with the marginal benefits percieved. The advantage of the benefit approach is that it enables the consumer to allocate resources for public goods[4] in the same way he is assumed to allocate resources for private goods; that is, by equating marginal costs with marginal benefits. Although the benefit approach provides an optimal solution at a conceptual level, it is extremely difficult to put into practice.[5] As a general statement, however, we can say we would want those who receive the benefits to be responsible for financing their costs.

For present purposes, it may be convenient to distinguish among three main groups of benefits:

    (1)   benefits which go to the individual being educated (or his family)—i.e., private benefits;

    (2)   benefits which go to members of the community in which the individual being educated resides; i.e., intracommunity benefits;

    (3)   benefits which go to members of other communities—i.e., intercommunity benefits.

In establishing an appropriate system of inter-governmental grants, our concern is primarily with the third. In order to establish a full system of benefit taxation, however, one would need to enumerate and quantify the private benefits, the spillovers, and the geographic extent of the spillovers. Having determined this, one could then determine the proportion of costs which "ought"[6] to come from the individual, the community, the county, the state, and the nation.

Spillovers from Education

Some of the more important spillovers from education are as follows:

(1) a more informed electorate and increased civic participation;
(2) increased productivity of an individual as a result of having highly educated coworkers;
(3) reduction in law enforcement needs;
(4) reduction in welfare costs;[7]
(5) reduction in unemployment compensation;
(6) greater tax contributions as a result of increased earning power of the individual.

Two issues need to be considered in order to determine the appropriate type of intergovernmental grant for education. The first is the effect of additional (more and/or better) education on each of the spillovers. The second is determining who is likely to be the beneficiary of the spillover.

Some Empirical Evidence. There is some readily available empirical evidence which is at least indicative of the effects of education on the spillovers cited above. In terms of the informed electorate spillover, there is some evidence that voter participation is positively related to the educational level of the individual. Regarding the 1952 and 1956 presidential elections, it was found that for men over age 34 and living outside the South, voting participation was 60%, 78%, and 88% for those having a grade school, high school, and college education, respectively.[8] Statistics on the relationship between poverty and low educational levels are relatively abundant. For example, in 1962, 61% of families designated as poor (an annual income less than $3,000) were headed by an individual having eight or fewer years of education. Seventy-eight percent of poor families were headed by an individual with eleven or fewer years of education.[9] As might be expected, education is an important factor in terms of the occupational opportunities available to the individual. Morgan et al. report that 70% of "spending unit heads" with less than a high school education enter the labor force in semiskilled and unskilled occupations. Job stability is also related to education. For example, 34% of all persons with less than a high school education reported being unemployed at some time during the period 1955-1960. The corresponding figure for individuals reported as "high school graduates/some college" was 21%; the figure for individuals with a college degree was 7%.[10]

Complications. While there is evidence suggestive of the relationship between education and a variety of spillovers, there are many complications involved in quantifying the spillovers and in determining the beneficiaries.

Consider, for example, the informed electorate spillover. The relationship between education and voter behavior is only an indirect one. The individual in grade school or high school will not become a voter until some time in the future. While an individual may be an educated voter, whether or not he will be a well-informed voter depends on his awareness of the particular issues on the ballot at that time. In addition, most of the empirical evidence is limited to quantitative changes in participation, whereas our concern is also with qualitative changes. It is probably reasonable to assume, however, that the two are related.

The second issue to be considered involves the likely beneficiaries of the spillover. A priori, we know that some of the benefits must be national in scope—partly because some elections are national, and partly as a result of migration. In order to approximate the benefits likely to accrue to the local community, it would be necessary to make the following sort of calculation: *the effect of additional education on having a more informed electorate and increased civic participation* multiplied by *the probability the individual will reside in the locality in which he was educated* multiplied by *the importance of local elections relative to all other elections.* Similar calculations would have to be made for the other major units of government. The principal difficulty is that factors one and three do not lend themselves to meaningful quantification.

The complications resulting from migration apply to all of the spillovers, although the importance of migration depends upon the importance of the actual physical location of an individual or spatial relationship between individuals in terms of their being recipients of spillovers.[11] In order to estimate the impact of migration on the beneficiaries of spillovers from education, it would be necessary to consider the residence of individuals at some initial time (e.g., when the education is being provided), the probability that both the individuals financing the education and the individuals receiving the education will be alive at some later time, and the future residence of both sets of individuals at some later time.[12] Moreover, migration itself appears to be related to education,[13] thereby complicating the estimation of future migration probabilities.

Given the close association between low educational attainment and poverty or frequency of unemployment, one might expect the potential reduction in welfare costs to be more important than most of the other spillovers listed earli-

er. There are two basic difficulties in using available statistics
to estimate the likely reduction in welfare costs resulting from
additional education. The first involves a question of causality. Low educational attainment is associated with poverty,
but this does not necessarily imply that they are causally
related. It is possible, in fact probable, that both are in part
the result of other factors, such as ability, motivation, educational background of parents, and so forth.[14] The second
difficulty is that any estimates regarding the expected reduction in welfare costs will be largely determined by projections
of future welfare programs and by the relationship between
education and employability likely to exist at some future
time. The following are illustrative of some of the problems
which result:

(a) The reduction in welfare costs depends in part on
     the level of welfare and on the extent of coverage
     in existence at any time. Our current public assis-
     tance programs are primarily designed to meet (or
     at least partially meet) the needs of only certain
     categories of the poor. One estimate indicated that
     only about one-third of the poor families and one-
     fourth of poor individuals (8 million out of 32
     million) received public assistance in 1965.[15] The
     expected reduction in welfare costs would depend
     on both the per recipient cost of welfare projected
     into the future and on the projected coverage of the
     program, neither of which is likely to be reflected
     in present welfare costs.

(b) Current figures indicating the relationship between
     educational attainment and unemployment or un-
     stable employment may be misleading with respect
     to future prospects for the poorly educated. Many
     members of the current labor force with low educa-
     tion entered the labor force at a time when the

average level of education was much lower than it is today. These individuals have now had twenty to thirty years during which to acquire a variety of skills. Employment opportunities for individuals currently entering the labor force with relatively little education appear to be limited. The unemployment rate for male dropouts (age 16-21) as of 1963, for example, was nearly twice as high as for young men who had graduated from high school.[16] Or, in other words, "the handicap imposed by a poor education is but a pale indication of what it will be in the future."[17]

(c) Determining the beneficiaries of a reduction in welfare costs is, in part, dependent on the method of financing in use at some particular time. If, for example, all welfare payments were financed at the national level, the benefits would be national and would increase as an individual's income increased (assuming federal expenditures are financed by a tax on income). In 1963, over 50% of state and local government expenditures on welfare were financed by the federal government, but over 30% were financed by state governments, with local governments financing the rest. In this situation, almost 50% of the benefits of a reduction in welfare costs would accrue to the state and local areas responsible for welfare payments—areas which may or may not have been responsible for the educational expenditures of the welfare recipients.

One other general problem is that much of the available statistical information is based on the level of educational attainment. This is no longer very relevant for primary and secondary education since the law requires children to remain in school until age 16 or 18. Even dollar expenditures would only approximate the desired information—partly because of differences in the costs of teachers' salaries, materials, and so forth and partly because the dollar amounts required to provide similar "levels" of education can be expected to differ among children, especially those representing societal extremes.

The difficulties in quantifying spillovers do not lessen the need for such information and a few attempts have been made in this direction.[18] In view of the problems mentioned above, one can question the usefulness of trying to quantify spillovers in order to justify specific expenditures by various levels of government. We can, however, establish the general structure of a system of intergovernmental grants which would compensate for spillovers, making use of the limited information available on spillovers in doing so.

Policy Implications

If external benefits are to be accounted for in the allocation of resources to education,[19] the general structure of the grant ought to be as follows:

(1) The grant should be categorical—in other words, the spending of the grant should be restricted to the particular program being subsidized.

(2) The grant should be a matching grant with the grantor's share of total expenditures approximating, to whatever extent is possible, the ratio of external benefits to total benefits existing at the margin.

In view of the available evidence regarding spillovers, it appears that grants for education should also possess the following characteristics:

(3) The grant should be inversely related to wealth.

379.122   W647a
c. 1

Wealth (expressed either in terms of income or property valuation) consistently has been found to be a major correlate of expenditures on education.[20] To the extent that one would expect the returns to education (including both internal and external benefits) to be greater at the margin where the expenditures are less, it would be appropriate to increase the size of the grant to the low wealth area relative to that of the high wealth area.[21] In addition, some of the spillovers appear to be particularly associated with children from low income families, given, for example, the greater tendency for dropouts to be from low income families and the expected future relationship between dropouts and frequency of unemployment and/or poverty.[22]

(4) At least a portion of the grant should be from the federal government. As noted, some of the spillovers are inherently national; others become national as a result of migration.

In summary, grants for education should be matching grants, inversely related to wealth, with a portion of the grant coming from the federal government. In view of the limited knowledge regarding the precise nature of the spillovers, one should note that the justification for an equalization grant on the basis of spillovers is somewhat weaker than the justification for the other characteristics of the grant outlined above.

INTERPERSONAL INCOME REDISTRIBUTION

A second effect of intergovernmental grants for education is on the distribution of income. Two main groups of individuals are of concern: the present generation of adults (especially the parents of public school children) and the future generation of adults (who are currently students).

Redistribution Among the Present Generation

Government[23] expenditures on education can be expected to affect the income of the present generation of adults both directly and indirectly. To the extent that the grant does not result in a net increase in educational expenditures, there is a direct effect on the community's income: the amount available for goods and services other than education is increased. To the extent that the grant increases the community's expenditures on education, there is an indirect effect on income in the form of an increased investment.[24] In a system where all taxpayers are taxed for educational expenditures, there will also be a shift in the distribution of real income in favor of parents relative to nonparents (or parents of nonpublic school children) and in favor of large families relative to small families. Whether or not government expenditures on education tend to equalize the distribution of real income depends on the distribution of benefits from educational expenditures among the various income brackets.[25]

Redistribution Among the Future Generation

The second and more important consideration is the use of educational expenditures as a means of redistributing income among the future generation. In other words, an alternative (or at least partial substitute) to the distribution of money income among an adult population would be to increase the educational expenditures for particular groups of children,[26] the implication being that education can be used to alter the future distribution of income. The correlation between education and income and the difficulties in isolating the differential properly attributable to education have already been mentioned. If it were possible to select a group of individuals who were similar in all relevant respects other than the quantity and quality of education received, then any differences in their earnings could be viewed as a result of differences in education. The difficulty is that there is some uncertainty regarding the relative importance of each of the "other relevant variables," in addition to problems in obtaining appropriate data. Several attempts have been made to estimate the impact of various levels of education on future income, although the results are difficult to compare.[27]

Considering educational expenditures as a means of redistributing income among the future generation focuses on the use of educational expenditures as an investment. In this case, a measure of major interest is the rate of return on the investment, since the latter takes account of differences in the costs of providing various levels of education, and also differences in the time horizons associated with the costs and benefits from education. Weisbrod[28] and Schultz,[29] for example, estimate the rate of return on primary education to be around 35%. Weisbrod[30] estimates the rate of return from high school (for males at age 17) to be around 14%. Hansen[31] estimates the rate of return from high school for the same group of individuals to be around 15%. Becker[32] estimates a higher rate of return from high school education, but his estimate is based on the "private" rate of return calculated at age 25. However, all of the authors express some warning about using their specific figures for policy purposes.

Our concern in this section is with the use of educational expenditures in changing the distribution of income as an alternative to changing the distribution at a later time by means of money transfers. To the extent that the rate of return from primary and secondary expenditures is greater than that obtainable elsewhere, the former is an economically more efficient way of achieving the desired change in the distribution of income. The above figures were not cited in order to establish whether or not this is the case, but rather to suggest the relevance of such considerations. Aside from efficiency considerations, using the leverage provided by education to change the distribution of income may be better than money income transfers because of the personal indignities frequently associated with the receipt of welfare payments.

Policy Implications

Redistribution Among the Present Generation. Attempting to redistribute income among the present generation by means of a grant to education is a poor "second-best" solution. If it is assumed that the grant increases educational expenditures, the redistribution is in the form of income-in-kind. Like all distributions of income-in-kind, redistribution by means of expenditures on education interferes with the allocation of resources determined by the market system and results in an "excess burden" similar to that associated with excise taxation.[33] Income redistribution by means of educational expenditures would also discriminate severely against low income individuals who have no children or whose children do not attend public schools.

If the grant is used to free local resources, the excess burden issue is no longer relevant, but the grant is unlikely to be effective in terms of redistribution. The reason is twofold. The first reason is that expenditures on education represent a small fraction of income. In Michigan, for example, total operating expenditures on education have averaged around 5% of income with the state's share averaging about half of the total.[34] An equalization grant involving something less than 2½% of income does not provide sufficient leverage to affect appreciably the distribution of income. The second reason is that the grant is given to a unit of government, in this case the school district, within which variations in income may be as great as or greater than variations between such governmental units. Furthermore, if the grant is used to free local resources, it is no longer a grant to education.

If redistribution to the present generation is an objective, the most effective way of accomplishing this objective is by means of cash transfers at the personal level. The use of cash transfers eliminates the excess burden associated with income-in-kind transfers. Operating at the personal level rather than at a district or municipal level provides far greater flexibility in reaching the individuals who are of concern. Similar objectives can be accomplished, although less effectively, through the use of unconditional or untied grants (that is, a grant which can be spent for any purpose).[35] The use of unconditional grants for distributional purposes may be justified if it is not feasible to redistribute at the personal level or if there are substantial limitations on mobility.[36]

Thus distribution objectives can be accomplished either by interpersonal transfers or by unconditioned grants. However, redistribution among the present generation cannot be accomplished effectively by means of an intergovernmental grant to education. Furthermore, attempting to use the grant for this purpose results in a grant which is ineffective both in terms of redistribution and as an aid to education.

Redistribution Among the Future Generation. In contrast to the case of the present generation, grants to education can be used as a means of redistributing income among the future generation. The reason is that the direct effect on income occurs (or is assumed to occur) because of the increase in education rather than in place of the increase in education.

Given the importance of community wealth in determining educational expenditures and assuming some causality between education and income, the implication of a redistributive objective is to increase expenditures in low wealth communities. In terms of the general structure of grants outlined earlier, this would increase the relative importance of the equalization portion of the matching grant.

CONCLUSIONS

In establishing a framework for intergovernmental grants to education, two basic issues are of concern: allocative efficiency, and interpersonal income redistribution. Because of the external benefits which result from education, a market-determined allocation of resources to education would be less than optimal. Intergovernmental grants are needed because some of the benefits are likely to accrue to individuals who (presently) reside outside the local school district. Allocative efficiency requires the use of a matching grant with the grantor's share of total expenditures equal to the ratio of external benefits to internal benefits existing at the margin. Although there are many difficulties in attempting to quantify the spillovers from education, there is some evidence that the grant should be inversely related to wealth with a portion of the grant coming from the federal government.

Grants to education also affect the distribution of income among both the present and future adult generations. The present generation is affected indirectly, by increasing its investment, and/or directly, by freeing local resources. However, if redistribution among the present generation is an objective, the appropriate instruments are either interpersonal cash transfers or unconditional grants. Grants to education are not appropriate. The effect on the future generation is due to the increased income associated with additional education. In this case, the grant is expected to affect future income and can be used for this purpose. Having future income redistribution via education as an objective increases the relative importance of the equalization portion of the matching grant.

Throughout this chapter, it has been either implicitly or explicitly concluded that the federal government is to play a major role within the system of grants to education—because of the spillovers associated with education and to the extent that educational expenditures are being used for distributional purposes. The role of the federal government in primary and secondary education until 1964 was negligible and at the present time is still minimal. Financial responsibility for primary and secondary education historically has been delegated to the states. In evaluating the state aid program in Michigan we will be making use of the general structure established in this chapter. The structure is applied to a state program rather than to a federal-state program as a reflection of political reality. This does not obviate the need for participation by the federal government.

NOTES TO CHAPTER 1

(All works referred to may be found in the Bibliography at the end of the book.)

1. For a concise statement of the identity between the perfectly competitive equilibrium solution and welfare maximization, see Henderson and Quandt (1959), Chapter 7.

2. In general, the existence of benefit spillovers implies that the market allocation of resources to the commodity in question will be less than optimal. An exception to this generality is discussed in Buchanan and Kafolgis (1963): 408-412.

3. For other listings of spillovers from education see Hirsch et al. (1964): 263; and Weisbrod (1964): 117.

4. A good is a public good to the extent that it results in benefit (cost) spillovers and a private good to the extent that it results in benefits which can be appropriated by any one individual. A "pure public" good would be one where none of the benefits can be appropriated by an individual.

5. For a discussion of the major difficulty, commonly referred to as the "revealed preference problem," see Musgrave (1959): 10-12.

6. "Ought"—relative to allocative efficiency. The latter obviously is not the only objective which needs to be considered with respect to the financing of education.

7. Since welfare costs involve transfer payments (rather than a net change in the amount of resources available to society) one can

question the propriety of including a reduction in welfare costs as a spillover. If, however, one assumes some sort of established distributional policy, e. g., that the nation as a whole has decided that those unable to provide for themselves will be supported to some degree by the rest of society, then a reduction in welfare costs can be regarded as a spillover from education.

8. Campbell et al. (1960): 495. Also cited in Break (1967): 64.

9. *Economic Report of the President* (1964).

10. Morgan et al. (1962): Chapter 23.

11. For example, if all welfare payments were financed at the federal level, then the physical location of potential welfare recipients would be irrelevant as far as identifying the beneficiaries of a reduction in welfare costs.

12. For an interesting attempt to develop population migration rate probability matrices and an application of the resulting migration model to empirical data, see Hirsch et al. (1964): 274-286 and appendix.

13. Fein (1965): 110-111; and Weisbrod (1964): 48.

14. There have been several attempts to estimate the increase in income or lifetime earnings attributable to education. The findings of some of these studies are briefly considered in the second section of Chapter 1.

15. Green and Lampman (1967): 133.

16. While the average dropout is younger than the average young graduate, this was cited as not being the major reason for the difference in employment rates. The rate of unemployment among dropouts declines somewhat after the first few years, but it remains much higher than among high school graduates. See *Manpower Report of the President* (1966): 93.

17. *Ibid.*: 96.

18. See, for example, Hirsch et al. (1964): 323-333, 338-341, 352-364; and Weisbrod (1964): 71-79, 84, 91-93.

19. By focusing on intergovernmental grants, we are implicitly assuming that the system of financing in use locally at least approximates a tax based on the local demand for education (in other words, is consistent with private benefits and intracommunity spillovers). This is not true in Michigan or elsewhere and this absence of benefit taxation is expected to influence the amount of resources devoted to education.

20. See, for example, Bishop (1964); and James et al. (1963): 75-85.

21. The rate of return appears to be greater in the South, where expenditures on education and educational attainment tend to be lower, thus providing some support for this point. See Weisbrod (1964): 134; and Becker and Chiswick (1966): 367-368.

22. A boy 16-17 years old from a family whose annual income is less than $3,000 is two and one-half times as likely to be a dropout as a boy whose family income is greater than $7,000. See *Manpower Report of the President* (1966): 93. While there is some evidence that educational attainment of parents is even more critical than income, parents' income is not a bad proxy for their education.

23. At the present time, "government" expenditures are predominantly state and local government expenditures. Estimated federal government expenditures on primary and secondary education for fiscal 1967 equaled $1.5 billion. State and local school expenditures by the state of Michigan for fiscal 1965 equaled $1.06 billion. See U. S. Bureau of the Budget (1966): 129 and Michigan, State of [1] : 5.

24. The way in which various types of grants can be expected to influence a district's expenditures on education is discussed in Chapter 5.

25. On the basis of the 1956 Michigan data, Musgrave and Daicoff estimated that expenditure benefits from primary and secondary education tended to rise, up to the $5,000–$7,000 income bracket, and then decline thereafter. See Musgrave and Daicoff (1958), tables 11-12. In terms of a more general analysis, the effect on the distribution of income depends on the net effect of taxes minus expenditures rather than on the expenditure side alone. It is possible, for example, that a distribution of educational benefits which favors lower income groups could be more than offset by a sufficiently regressive system of taxation. The Musgrave-Daicoff study also contains an estimate of the net effect of taxes minus expenditures by income classes in Michigan. *Ibid.*: tables 8, 11-14. For an indication of the impact of a proportional income tax on the state tax structure relative to the distribution otherwise obtained, see *Ibid.*, table 8. Since the recently adopted income tax was added to most of the existing taxes, an estimate of the current tax distribution would need to include all of the taxes listed in table 8, exclusive of the Business Activities Tax, with proper weights assigned to reflect the relative importance of each of the taxes.

26. Under our present system of financing education, this would imply increasing the expenditures of a particular school or school district. Increasing the expenditures for an entire school is likely to be effective for large city schools, since the latter tend to be relatively homogeneous with respect to the social and economic background of the student population. This approach may not be very effective for smaller communities, which tend to have one or few schools, and in which student populations may be very heterogeneous in terms of background.

27. Major difficulties in comparison are due to the differences in the "effect of education" being measured; e.g., value of additional lifetime income (from all primary and secondary education or different levels of it), present value of additional lifetime income or of additional annual income (from all primary and secondary education or the average effect of an additional year or different levels) and also because of differences in the costs included. For a discussion of some of the measurements which have been used and the implications of using each of them, see Hansen (1963): 128-140.

28. Weisbrod (1964): 14.

29. Schultz (1961): 81.

30. Weisbrod (1964): 140.

31. Hansen (1963): 138.

32. Becker (1964): 128.

33. Musgrave (1959): 140-154.

34. As of the mid-1960s, local expenditures on education averaged around 2.5 % of income, with slightly less than half of school (operating) costs being financed locally. See Barlow (1967): 3, and Michigan School Finance Study (1967): 18.

35. The idea of an unconditional grant between governmental units was suggested by Walter W. Heller in 1964.

36. If there is a substantial amount of immobility, differences in fiscal capacity between local governmental units also need to be considered in formulating distributional policies. This is because of the interdependence of income with respect to the cost of providing public goods. In other words, the amount of public goods available to an individual at a given level of taxes depends on the taxable wealth of all the individuals within the community. This, in turn, means that a low income individual in a community of low taxable wealth is in a worse position

than a low income individual in a community of high taxable wealth. If there are no limitations on mobility, it can be assumed that differences in fiscal capacity are taken into account in choosing one's place of residence. If there are limitations on mobility, compensation for fiscal inequalities can be made through the use of unconditional grants as long as differences in fiscal capacity are not fully capitalized. However, compensation can also be made at the personal level.

OBJECTIVES OF THE MICHIGAN PROGRAM

Thus far we have considered state aid to education in terms of economic theory. In Chapter 2 we examine the expressed or implied objectives of the existing Michigan program of aid to education and some of the implications of these objectives, which, of course, are social as well as economic. Since the concept of the foundation program provides the social philosophy underlying the Michigan program and those of most other states, we shall begin the discussion at this point.

THE FOUNDATION PROGRAM

Objective

The concept of the foundation program was developed by Strayer and Haig in the early 1920s.[1] Its basic assumption is that the state has the responsibility of assuring that an "adequate education" be made available for all children in the state. The primary objective is generally stated as "equalizing educational opportunity." This equality of educational opportunity usually has not meant to imply identical education for all children, but rather equalizing at some level regarded as being "adequate to meet the needs of the people." Thus "adequacy" is used to define the program, and its objective is to assure that an adequate education is made available.[2]

Framework

Within the framework of the foundation program, discussion has centered on three issues: the structure of the program, the state's share of the program, and the manner in which the level of the program is established.

Structure of the Program. Two approaches have been suggested regarding the structure of the program. The first is the "fixed-unit" or "unit" grant developed by Strayer and Haig. This plan is the one which has been adopted by almost all of the states, including Michigan. The alternative to the unit grant is the percentage grant. A variant of the percentage plan was initially proposed by Updegraff in 1922. In its basic form the percentage plan corresponds to the matching grant described in Chapter 1. Under it the state pays some percentage of the sum financed locally.[3]

Under the unit grant, the state government establishes a unit cost and then pays some portion of that unit cost. The total grant from the state becomes its share of the unit cost times the number of units. The distinguishing feature of the unit grant is that if the local government spends more than its share of the determined unit cost all of the additional expenditures are financed locally.

State's Share of the Program. The concept of the foundation program is credited with providing a "clear-cut division between state responsibility and local responsibility."[4] A general statement frequently made about the division is that the state should "equalize the local tax burden and the amount of local support."[5] Reference is then usually made to the program developed by Strayer and Haig. Under their system, once the unit cost is established, a tax rate is calculated which is sufficient to finance the program in the "richest" districts. The same tax rate is applied to all other communities. Since other communities have less taxable capacity, the revenue produced by the tax would be insufficient to cover the established unit cost. The state grant provides the difference between the amount produced by the tax rate which has been set in the richest districts and the unit cost multiplied by the number of units.[6]

The general formula used in the distribution of state aid under the unit grant is therefore as follows:

(need)	gross allowance per pupil (or unit cost)
(local fair share)	minus deductible millage times the per pupil valuation of property in the district

---

(equalization)	state aid payments per pupil to the district

In the Strayer and Haig plan, the deductible millage is the rate required to finance the program in the richest districts. Their plan did not indicate how the gross allowance or unit cost is to be established.

Establishing the Level. The manner in which the appropriate unit is determined is a matter of major concern. Once the unit cost is established, the level of the foundation program is also established; If the unit cost is less than the amount needed to provide an adequate education, then the state cannot fulfill the objective of assuring the provision of an adequate education.

Two approaches have been suggested for determining the unit cost. One is by a "dollars per unit of need"; that is, establishing some dollar per pupil figure needed to provide an adequate education. The second approach is in terms of "services and facilities needed." In this case, an attempt is made to establish the services needed to provide an adequate education, such as some desired pupil-teacher ratio, number of specialists, pupils per classroom, and so forth. Once the necessary services have been determined, an estimate of the cost of providing these services can be made. Logically, the two approaches are the same. The first focuses on cost, but implicitly assumes that a fixed number of dollars per pupil will provide an adequate level of services. The second approach seems preferable since it focuses attention on the services deemed necessary to provide an adequate education and should make it easier to judge whether the objective of the program is being fulfilled.[7] The major issue which remains, however, is specifying the services (and their dollar equivalent) needed to provide an adequate education.

OBJECTIVES IN MICHIGAN

In Michigan, a major portion of the state program is a foundation program. Distribution is by means of a unit grant with the unit expressed in terms of a uniform number of dollars per pupil.

When specific objectives of the Michigan program are spelled out, the acceptance of the foundation philosophy is clear. An Educational Finance Study Commission appointed by former Governor Williams, for example, regarded the following to be the main objectives of the Michigan program:

(a) The state is responsible for insuring that every child has an adequate program of education.

(b) Education is a joint responsibility of the state and the local school districts, with the actual program being carried out by the local districts.

(c) Local districts must make an equitable financial effort to support their own programs.

(d) The state should underwrite differences between the amount needed for a foundation program and the amount provided locally from an equitable financial effort.

(e) The district's eligibility for state aid should depend both on its fiscal ability and on its tax rate.

(f) Districts should be permitted and encouraged to spend more than their share of the foundation program.

(g) The distribution formula should assure greater equalization of educational opportunity.

(h) An objective measure of educational need should be used.

(i) The program should be easy to administer and should provide enough stability to permit effective planning.[8]

Let us examine more closely some of the objectives of the Michigan program and their implications.

Equalizing Educational Opportunity

There are occasional references in the education literature regarding the need to compensate for differences in other local government needs.[9] This appears to reflect some confusion as to whether the objective is: (1) equalizing the resources available for education, or (2) equalizing the educational services provided. Although these interpretations to some extent are related, they have very different implications. If the emphasis on equal educational opportunity is in terms of resource availability, then the issue is one of redistributing income among the adult generation. As outlined in Chapter 1, this is neither a very feasible nor appropriate objective for a grant to education. The second interpretation, equalizing educational services, is the one usually implied and for present purposes is assumed to be the relevant interpretation. It could still be argued that one reason why educational opportunities would be unequal is that areas differ in their resource availability. However, in this case the emphasis is on altering the education provided rather than the resources available for education.

When educational opportunity is being defined in terms of the educational services provided, equal opportunity implies an equal level of the purchased inputs which make up the educational services. If there are variations in the costs of these inputs (teachers, materials, etc.), the provision of a uniform dollar figure per pupil is unlikely to result in equal educational opportunity. For example, it may cost more for a poor or "disadvantaged" area to hire a teacher of some given quality than it does a wealthy or "advantaged" area. No attempt is made in this study to estimate the different dollar expenditures needed in various areas of Michigan in order to equalize opportunity. Although expenditure figures are frequently cited in later chapters as if equal expenditures represented equal educational opportunity, we recognize that different expenditures may be needed to provide equal educational services.

Although an equal dollar expenditure does not necessarily imply an equal educational opportunity, a recent study of the Michigan educational system does indicate a direct relationship between per pupil expenditures and educational opportunity. Educational opportunity (frequently referred to as "quality of education") was defined in terms of educational programs and class size, qualifications and allocation of teachers, instructional equipment and materials, and so forth.[10] Given this finding and similar findings elsewhere, expenditures figures are also cited in a later chapter as if higher expenditures are associated with a higher quality of education. At the same time, it is acknowledged that an increase in quality can occur without an increase in expenditures and that an increase in expenditures does not necessarily imply an increase in quality.[11]

Equalization—Adequacy

The primary objective of the foundation program is frequently stated as "equalizing educational opportunity," which is then defined as equalizing in terms of an adequate education. The 1956 statement of Michigan objectives also mentions both the provision of an adequate education and (greater) equalization of educational opportunity.

The terms equalization, adequacy, and equalizing in terms of adequacy are used ambiguously. Equalizing educational opportunity implies the removal of any differences in the availability of educational services. Using the term adequate in this context presumably refers to the level at which the equalization is to occur. However, the statement "equalizing in terms of an adequate education" is of limited value since there are likely to be large variations in what individuals regard as being adequate. As an example, the Superintendent of Public Instruction defined adequacy of educational opportunity as requiring "sufficient support to make it possible for every child to develop every capacity to his maximum potential."[1][2] This is an unusual definition of adequacy and probably goes beyond the sentiments of the legislature or the people of the state.

Attempting to justify the level of the foundation program in terms of adequacy is likely to represent an exercise in futility. However, it is clear that unless adequacy is considered at least equal to the highest level of expenditures any district would be willing to spend, or unless districts are not allowed to spend more than the foundation program, equalizing in terms of adequacy will not result in equal educational opportunity. Neither of these conditions reflects the apparent intent of the program. What seems to be implied is that the foundation program should be set at a level which is high enough to avoid socially or politically unacceptable discrepancies in educational opportunity. This obviously does not specify the appropriate level of the foundation program, but it is less ambiguous than the concept of adequacy. Justifying the particular level at which to equalize will have to be done on the basis of criteria other than those provided by the foundation program. The objective of avoiding large discrepancies in educational opportunity does suggest, however, that the foundation program should be set at least equal to average expenditures.[13]

Potential Conflicts

Some of the objectives expressed by the Educational Finance Study Commission are or may be conflicting. For example, "encouraging" expenditures beyond the level set by the foundation program may conflict with an approximation of equal educational opportunity. Equalizing educational opportunity may also conflict with the preservation of "local control" (depending on how the latter is defined). Establishing priorities among some objectives can be done on the basis of efficiency considerations; others will depend on value judgments. In evaluating the present program in terms of its own objectives, we shall proceed on the assumption that the primary objective is the equalization of educational opportunity.

CONCLUSIONS

The Michigan program is based on the concept of a foundation program. The primary objective of the foundation program is to equalize educational opportunity, which is then defined as equalizing in terms of an adequate education. The distribution of state aid within the framework of a foundation program is almost always on the basis of a unit grant. Under a unit grant the state establishes a unit cost, which in turn establishes the level of the foundation program, and then pays some portion of it. The state's share is inversely related to the district's per pupil property valuation. Under the Strayer and Haig plan, the deductible millage, which is the tax rate used in ćalculating the local share of the unit cost, is set so that the richest districts finance the entire unit cost.

The primary objective of the Michigan program basically is that of the foundation program. To avoid the ambiguity involved with the concept of an adequate education, the equalization objective is interpreted to mean that the foundation program should be set at a high enough level to avoid socially or politically unacceptable discrepancies in educational opportunity. This suggests that the program should be set at least equal to average expenditures. Other objectives include the encouragement of expenditures beyond the level of expenditures established by the state, an equitable financial effort on the part of the local districts, maintenance of local control (with some qualifications), and so forth. Because the fulfillment of some of the objectives may infringe on the fulfillment of other objectives, it will be necessary to establish or assume priorities among objectives.

In the remaining chapters, the Michigan program is evaluated both in terms of the expressed or implied objectives of the state program and in terms of the general framework developed in Chapter 1. Evaluating the program in terms of its own objectives basically implies evaluating the program as a foundation program. For this part of the evaluation, both the objectives and the structural framework of the foundation program are accepted as given.

NOTES TO CHAPTER 2

1. Strayer and Haig (1924): 173-175.
2. For further discussion of the concept of the foundation pro-

gram and usage of the term "equality of educational opportunity," see Mort et al. (1960): Chapters 2 and 3.

3. Benson (1963): 316.

4. Mort et al. (1960): Chapter 11.

5. *Ibid.*; and Burke (1957): 485.

6. Strayer and Haig (1924): 204.

7. Johns and Morphit (1963): Chapter 36.

8. Michigan Educational Finance Study Commission (1956): 2-3.

9. See, for example, Lindman (1964): 1-5.

10. Michigan Educational Finance Study Commission (1956): 4-6.

11. If, for example, there are economies of scale in the provision of educational services, district consolidation would result in a higher quality of education for a given level of expenditures. Although it is reasonable to assume there are some economies of scale in education, little work has been done in this area.

12. Michigan, State of [8] : 50.

13. Making this an operational guide would require using the average expenditures of the preceding period.

THE CURRENT MICHIGAN PROGRAM

Chapter 3 focuses on the current Michigan program of aid to education. The first two sections briefly review the changes in the financing of state expenditures on education and describe the current program. The remainder of the chapter is concerned with the foundation program portion of the state aid program. The topics considered include: the changes in the components of the foundation program; the implications of these components, and their changes on the distribution of state aid among school districts; and an evaluation of the Michigan program as a foundation program.

FINANCING STATE AID TO EDUCATION

A brief description of the way in which state aid has been financed is presented below. The primary concern of this study is with the expenditure side of the "current program" of state aid to education.[1] The main reason for reviewing the system of financing state aid is that the distinguishing characteristic of the current program involved a legal change in the financing.

Prior to the Current Program

Studies by Betty Tableman and John Sly et al. provide historical reviews and some analysis of the financing and distribution of state aid in Michigan up until the early 1950s.[2] The main point for present purposes is that until the current program, state expenditures on education were dependent on the previous year's (or years') revenue collections of certain taxes earmarked for education.

As of the early 1950s, one-sixth of the yield from the sales tax, plus 44.77% of the yield of the sales tax from the "second next preceding year," plus the yield from the Primary School Interest Fund, was earmarked for education.[3] Having sales tax collections in one year form the basis of appropriations in the next year of an amount to be disbursed in the third year, irrespective of the state's fiscal position in the second and third years, leads to some obvious problems during an economic downturn. This problem was remedied when disbursements were put on a current basis, effective for fiscal 1955. At the same time, a separate School Aid Fund was established, with two-thirds of the revenue from the state sales tax to be used to finance the fund.[4] In fiscal 1958, the revenue from a one mill cigarette tax and a four percent liquor excise tax was earmarked for education and included in the School Aid Fund.[5] Despite these additions, the revenue from the School Aid Fund and the Primary School Interest Fund was insufficient to finance the foundation program enacted by the legislature for fiscal 1958. Believing that the state was morally obligated to meet the full provisions of the program, the legislature passed a Supplementary State Aid Appropriations Act which financed the additional amount from General Fund revenue.[6] This occurred again in fiscal 1959. During 1959, the legislature amended the School Aid Appropriations Act, instructing the state to appropriate from the General Fund the amount needed to offset any deficiencies in the School Aid Fund.[7]

Under the Current Program

The independence of state expenditures on education

from the taxes earmarked for education, incorporated into the basic appropriations act in 1959, represents the onset of the current program. Although the earmarking of particular tax yields has continued, it can now be regarded as a formality with few or no implications for the financing of educational expenditures.

Some additional changes regarding the earmarked taxes for education have occurred during the course of the current program. The new state constitution (1963) has earmarked one-half of the sales tax yield for the School Aid Fund.[8] The same portion of the cigarette tax and liquor excise previously earmarked by statute has been continued. A second change was the elimination of the Primary School Interest Fund. The revenue from the seven taxes which previously went into the fund is now classified as part of General Fund, General Purpose revenue (as opposed to General Fund, Special Purpose).

DESCRIPTION OF THE CURRENT PROGRAM

The Michigan program of aid to education is composed of two main parts: a foundation program and a variety of special grants. The dollar amounts spent by the state on primary and secondary education for the period fiscal 1960 to fiscal 1966 are shown in Table 1. The expenditures listed under IA are usually listed as special grants, but since they are essentially equalization grants they have been included as a subsection of the foundation program. The same expenditures are given in percentage terms in Table 2.

Components of the Current Program

State Share of Equalization: The state share for any district equals the difference between the gross allowance times the number of pupils, and the "deductible millage"

TABLE 1

STATE EXPENDITURES FOR PRIMARY AND SECONDARY EDUCATION FOR FISCAL YEARS 1960–1966

	1960	1961	1962	1963	1964	1965	1966
	(in millions of dollars except where noted otherwise)						
I Foundation program							
State share of equalization	260.1	262.9	273.7	304.3	315.9	341.6	377.3
Additional aid for low valuation							23.2
IA Expenditures relating to equalization							
Hardship aid ("Aid to financially distressed districts")	3.0	2.8	3.0	6.4	7.2	8.4	.3
High tax levy waiver						.4	3.0
II Special grants							
Tuition and transportation	14.8	14.8	15.0	13.5	13.5	15.5	18.5
Special education[a]	8.6	10.0	11.2	12.1	13.0	15.7	21.3
Retirement	33.7	38.5	40.9	39.8	43.1	53.2	68.8
Other[b]	1.1	1.8	2.1	2.3	2.0	2.2	6.4
Total expenditures	321.3	330.8	345.9	378.4	394.7	437.0	518.4
Number of pupils (000's)	1624.3	1676.4	1733.7	1794.0	1856.9	1917.9	1968.4
Expenditure per pupil	$198	$197	$203	$211	$213	$228	$263

a. Includes county trainables aid.

b. Other includes vocational education, intermediate district aid, special aid for underpriviledged (fiscal 1966), etc.

SOURCES: "Citizens Research Council Comments," and Michigan, State of *Detail of State Operations and Local Benefits Budgets for Fiscal Years 1960–1966.*

TABLE 2

PERCENTAGE DISTRIBUTION OF STATE EXPENDITURES FOR PRIMARY AND SECONDARY EDUCATION FOR FISCAL YEARS 1960–1966

		1960	1961	1962	1963	1964	1965	1966
I	Foundation program							
	State share of equalization	81.0	79.5	79.1	80.4	80.4	78.2	72.8
	Additional aid for low valuation							4.5
IA	Expenditures relating to equalization							
	Hardship aid ("Aid to financially distressed districts")	.9	.8	.9	1.7	1.8	1.9	.1
	High tax levy waiver						.1	.6
II	Special grants							
	Tuition and transportation	4.6	4.5	4.3	3.6	3.4	3.5	3.6
	Special education	2.7	3.0	3.2	3.2	3.3	3.6	4.1
	Retirement	10.5	11.6	11.8	10.5	10.9	12.2	13.3
	Other	.3	.5	.6	.6	.5	.5	1.2
	Total expenditures[a]	100	100	100	100	100	100	100

a. Detail may not add to total due to rounding.

times the district's property valuation. Equalization expenditures increased from around $260 million to over $400 million[9] between fiscal 1960 and fiscal 1966, an increase of 54%. Part of this merely reflects an increase in the number of public school students—from around 1.6 million to almost 2 million, an increase of 21%. During this period, foundation program expenditures have accounted for about 80% of state expenditures on education.

Hardship Aid: Additional aid is provided for low valuation districts which fulfill certain requirements. (For example, the district must have a total tax levy of at least 20 mills, with no more than 13 mills being used for debt retirement.) In general, the amount of hardship aid is determined by the millage levied above 20 mills but under 31 mills and by the district's property valuation. The aid is positively related to millage levied and negatively related to the district's property valuation. The specific amount of aid received is determined by a rather complicated formula.[10] Expenditures for hardship aid represent a minor fraction of total expenditures, i.e., less than 2%. In 1966, an optional foundation program was offered to low valuation districts as an alternative to hardship aid. The sharp decline in hardship aid in 1966 indicates that the optional foundation program was more advantageous for almost all low valuation districts relative to hardship aid.

High Tax Levy Waiver: On the assumption that districts which levy above average tax rates for purposes other than school operating expenditures are less able to finance their school expenditures, special aid has been granted to high tax districts. The aid is limited to districts with an average total tax levy (minus school operating levy) greater than 125% of the average in the state. Districts meeting the requirement have their valuation reduced for purposes of state aid. (Since the state's share is negatively related to the district's valuation, a reduction in valuation increases the state's share and therefore state aid.) The increase in aid between 1965 and

1966 reflects the removal of the $.4 million ceiling established in 1965.[11]

Tuition and Transportation: Tuition allowances are given to the "receiving" district with the amount granted depending on the receiving district's minimum rate per pupil. As of fiscal 1963, the limit for tuition grants was set at $500,000.[12] Expenditures in the preceding year were slightly less than $3 million. The introduction of the ceiling accounts for the decline in expenditures between 1962 and 1963. Transportation allowances for regular students are based on the number of students living one and a half miles from school and outside a municipality. The maximum amount granted per pupil has been set in either dollars or percentage of cost. Slightly different but similar allowances are provided for the transportation of handicapped and emotionally disturbed children. Total expenditures on transportation have been subject to various ceilings. The ceilings have been set at $12 million, $13 million, and $15 million as of fiscal 1959, 1962, and 1964, respectively. In fiscal 1965, the ceiling was set at 75% of cost.[13]

Special Education: Special education refers to the programs for the mentally and physically handicapped, and for emotionally disturbed children. Through 1966, aid was based on a weighted pupil and teacher allowance, with different weights and different teacher allowances assigned for various kinds of disabilities.[14] The relatively large increase in expenditures in 1966 reflects the extension of special education auxiliary services to parochial school children living in public school districts providing these services.[15]

Retirement: Retirement grants reflect the state's responsibility for financing retirement plans for public school employees. Two points are apparent from Tables 1 and 2. First, retirement grants represent the largest nonequalization expenditure—over 50% of the approximately 20% not spent on equalization. Second, there has been a substantial increase in retirement grants since 1964. Up to that time the state had been appropriating less than the amount needed to finance current retirement costs. The 1963 constitution required that retirement contributions be funded in the year they accrue and that these funds not be used to finance previously accrued liabilities.[16]

Other: The main components of this category are grants for vocational education, intermediate school districts, and, in 1966, "Special Aid for the Underprivileged." The latter was a $4 million grant and accounts for the relatively large increase in expenditures which occurred in 1966.

Requirements

The receipt of state aid is subject to certain requirements. These include the following:

(1) School is to be maintained for at least nine months.

(2) No allowance is received for pupils in excess of a pupil-teacher ratio of 34:1 for districts with at least 350 pupils. (Enforcement, however, is left to the discretion of the state superintendent.)

(3) Funds must be used for current operating expenses, but up to five percent can be used for Capital Outlay and Debt Retirement.

(4) Districts must levy a specified millage for operating purposes in order to receive their full amount of aid—frequently referred to as the "mandated portion" or "mandated millage." From 1959 through 1965, the mandated millage was 8 mills. Districts received a prorated reduction in their aid if they levied between 6 and 8 mills (i.e., if they levied 6 mills they received six-eighths of their full aid, and so forth). For 1966 the mandated millage was set at 9 mills and a prorated reduction was given for districts levying between 7 and 9 mills.[17]

THE FOUNDATION PROGRAM IN MICHIGAN

Our concern in this section is with the components of Michigan's foundation program, their movements from 1960 to 1966, and the implications of the components and their movements on the distribution of state funds.

Components of the Foundation Program

We begin by redefining each of the components of the foundation program. The "gross allowance" is the foundation program—that is, the minimum amount of expenditures assured available to all participating districts. It is supposed to represent the level of expenditures which will avoid unacceptable differences in educational opportunity. In Michigan the gross allowance is set in terms of dollars per pupil. (The total amount assured available in any district is therefore the dollars per pupil figure times the number of pupils.)

The "deductible millage" is the millage rate used in the distribution formula. The deductible millage times the district's (state-equalized) valuation[18] determines the "local fair share" which is the district's share of the foundation program. The difference between the gross allowance and the local share comes from the state as state aid.

The "mandated millage" is the millage (for operating purposes) which must be levied locally if the district is to receive its full amount of aid. If the district's levy is within a two mill range below the mandated millage, it receives a prorated reduction in state aid. If the district's levy is below the two mill range, it receives no state aid.

The gross allowance, deductible millage, and mandated millage for the years 1960-1966 are given in Table 3. The gross allowance remained at $205 for a three-year period. By 1966, it had increased to $255.[19] Similarly, the deductible millage remained at 3.25 mills for a three-year period. By 1966, it had increased to 4.6 mills. As already noted, the

TABLE 3

THE FOUNDATION PROGRAM IN MICHIGAN FOR THE FISCAL YEARS 1960–1966[a]

	1960	1961	1962	1963	1964	1965	1966 (A)	1966 (B)[b] Optional program for low valuation districts
Gross allowance ($ per pupil)	205	205	205	224	224	236.50	225	380
Deductible millage	3.25	3.25	3.25	3.875	3.875	4.25	4.6	14.5
Mandated millage	8	8	8	8	8	8	9	9

a. Separate foundation programs are available for one-teacher and two-teacher schools.

b. Payments under B were limited to $23,250,000 more than would be provided under A.

SOURCE: Michigan, State of *Detail of State Operations and Local Benefits Budgets for the Years 1960-1966.*

mandated millage remained at 8 mills until 1966, at which time it was raised to 9 mills.

Distribution of State Aid

The amount of state aid which any district receives is a function of the gross allowance, the deductible millage, and the district's property valuation. The function can be described by a straight line, $y = a - bX_n$, where y = state aid per pupil, a = the gross allowance per pupil, b = deductible millage, and X_n = state equalized valuation (SEV) per pupil in district n.

The distribution of state aid for the years 1960-1966 can thus be described by the following set of equations:

1960-62	$y = 205$	$- .00325X_n$
1963-64	$y = 224$	$- .003875X_n$
1965	$y = 236.50$	$- .00425X_n$
1966	$y = 255$	$- .0046X_n$ (Program A)

A graphic description of state aid for the period 1960-1966 is shown in Figure 1. The intercept of the line, "a," is given by the gross allowance. As can be seen from Figure 1, the line intersects the vertical axis at increasingly higher points, indicating that the level of the foundation program has been increasing over time. The negative sign in the equations means that the lines are downward sloping (which also means that the higher the district's SEV, the less state aid it receives). The slope of the line, "b," is determined by the deductible millage. As noted, the deductible millage has been increasing. This means that the lines are becoming steeper and the distribution of state aid therefore more "progressive."[20] It can also be seen that the lines intersect the horizontal axis at lower values over time. In other words, the district valuation at which state aid becomes zero has been declining. This in itself is of little significance. As of 1966,

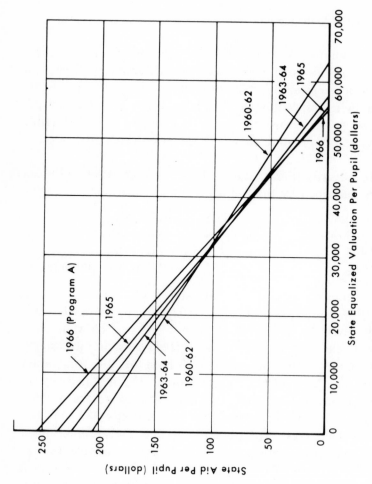

Figure 1   DISTRIBUTION OF STATE AID (FOUNDATION PROGRAM ONLY)

Fiscal 1960-66

state aid became zero only for districts with a per pupil SEV of at least \$55,435. Among K-12 districts (districts providing kindergarten through twelfth grade)[21] the highest per pupil SEV was at \$53,534.[22] In other words, everybody gets something. It is significant to note, however, that there has been a small decline in the absolute amount of state aid going to the districts with the highest valuations.

In 1966, an alternative foundation program (Program B) was made available for low valuation districts meeting certain requirements. Program B nominally provided for a gross allowance of \$380 and a deductible millage of 14.5 for districts having three or more teachers, sixty or more students, a local levy of at least 9 mills, and a per pupil SEV of less than \$12,600. It was a nominal provision because expenditures for Program B were limited to \$23,250,000 above what would have been spent under A, whereas the estimated cost of implementing B was \$36,000,000.[23] The limit on the additional expenditures is approximately two-thirds of the estimated cost. The state adjusted its expenditures by providing two-thirds of the additional aid provided by Program B relative to the amount of aid provided by Program A, plus the amount of aid due to the district from Program A. The distribution formula for districts eligible for Program B was therefore:

$$y = 2/3 \ [(380 - .0145X_n) - (255 - .0046X_n)] + 255 - .0046X_n$$

This is equivalent to:

$$y = 338.3 - .0112X_n$$

A graphic description of state aid in 1966 is shown in Figure 2. With the introduction of Program B, the distribution appears as a kinked line. The kink in the distribution occurs at the point where the distribution of state aid under Program B intersects the distribution under A. This occurs at an SEV of \$12,621. Since there were no districts with an SEV be-

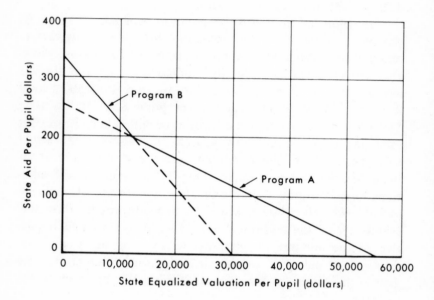

Figure 2   DISTRIBUTION OF STATE AID, 1966

tween $12,600 and $12,621, we can see there was no need to limit Program B to districts with an SEV of less than $12,600. Beyond this point it was in the district's own best interest to switch to A.

EVALUATION OF THE MICHIGAN PROGRAM AS A FOUNDATION PROGRAM

For part of our evaluation of the Michigan program, both the expressed objectives and the existing framework are accepted as given. Since the Michigan program is based on the concept of the foundation program, this implies an evaluation of the Michigan program as a foundation program.

The primary objective of the foundation program (and an expressed objective of the Michigan program) is the equalization of educational opportunity. This is interpreted to mean the avoidance of socially and politically unacceptable differences in the educational services made available. The avoidance of unacceptable differences is assumed to imply that the level of the foundation program should be set at least equal to average expenditures. A second concern within the concept of the foundation program is that of the local fair share. Aside from the Strayer and Haig criterion, there is little guidance as to what local share would be fair.[24] According to Strayer and Haig, the tax rate used in calculating the local share should be the tax rate needed to finance the entire foundation program in the richest districts.[25]

Equalization Relative to the Statutory Gross Allowance

From 1960 to 1962, the gross allowance was set at $205 per pupil. The 1966 program established a gross allowance of $255 per pupil for districts with a per pupil state equalized valuation of at least $12,600, and a gross allowance of $338 for districts with a per pupil SEV less than $12,600. In 1962, average per pupil operating expenditure (for all districts) was $375.66.[26] By 1966, average per pupil operating expenditure (for K-12 districts) had increased to $440.97.[27] As of 1962, the gross allowance represented slightly less than 55% of average operating expenditures. By 1966, the Program A gross allowance was slightly over 57% of average operating expenditures, the Program B gross allowance 76%.

The Michigan program thus appears to be closer to fulfilling the objective of a foundation program in 1966 than it was in 1962. The equalization is not yet set at the minimum level which avoids unacceptable differences in educational opportunity, assuming the minimum level is approximated by average expenditures. At this point, however, it is necessary to consider the deductible-mandated millage discrepancy.

Deductible Millage-Mandated Millage Discrepancy

Most foundation programs have two components; Michigan's has three. The additional one results from the use of one millage rate in the distribution formula and another millage rate as the requirement for participation in the program. The first point to note is that within the framework of a unit grant foundation program it is clearly inconsistent to have a mandated millage of, say, 8 mills and a deductible millage of, say, 3.25 mills. The objective of the foundation program is to assure a certain level of equalization of educational opportunity. Part of this assured level is to come from local districts, part from the state. Whatever share represents the local fair share in terms of distributing state aid by implication should be the required millage for participation.

The discrepancy, however, does more than just represent an inconsistency in the program. The "effective gross allowance" (the minimum per pupil assured available to all participating districts) is the statutory figure only for a district with zero property valuation. For all other districts, the effective

1965 $y = 236.50 + (.008 - .00425)X_n$

1966 $y = 255 \quad + (.009 - .0046)X_n$

Graphs of the equations are shown in Figure 3. As long as the deductible millage is less than the mandated millage, the line slopes upward. Until 1966, the lines were becoming flatter, reflecting the fact that the deductible millage had been increasing during a time when the mandated millage had remained constant. This was not true for the effective gross allowance of Program A in 1966. The deductible millage had again increased, but the mandated millage had increased more —thus widening the discrepancy between the two.

As can be seen from Figure 4, the introduction of Program B in 1966 altered the pattern of the effective gross allowance. In this case, the effective gross allowance slopes downward as long as Program B is operative ($y = 338.3 - .0022X_n$) and then slopes upward when Program A takes over. The reason is still due to the discrepancy between the deductible millage and the mandated millage.

Equalization Relative to the Effective Gross Allowance

In view of the discrepancy between the statutory and effective gross allowance, it is necessary to reconsider briefly the degree to which the Michigan program fulfills the objective of a foundation program.

Considering districts with a per pupil valuation of $1,000 and $40,000 as indicative of the extremes, the minimum amount per pupil assured available varied between $209.75 and $395.00, $228.13 and $389, $240.25and $386.50, and $336.10 and $431.00 for the fiscal years 1960-62, 1963-64, 1965, and 1966. The amount assured available for a more representative district of, say, $12,600, in each of the same years was $264.85, $275.98, $283.75, and $310.44.

If we again use average expenditures as the minimum for providing an "acceptable" degree of equalization, the Michi-

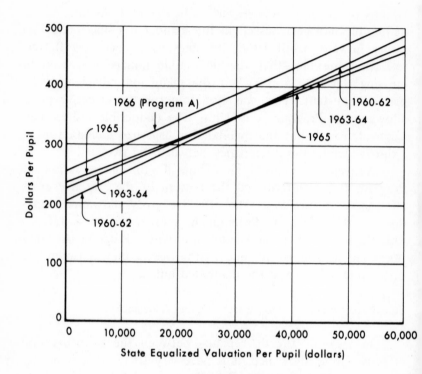

Figure 3   "EFFECTIVE GROSS ALLOWANCE"

Fiscal 1960-66

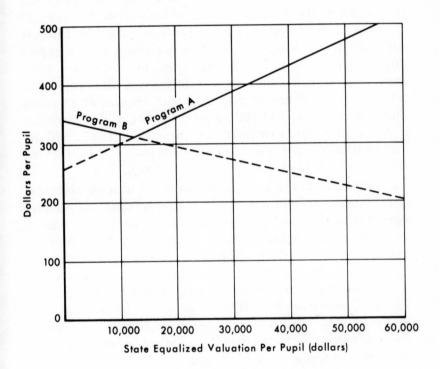

Figure 4   "EFFECTIVE GROSS ALLOWANCE" 1966

gan program approaches fulfillment of the objective of a foundation program for districts with the highest per pupil valuation. Except for 1966, the lower the district's valuation, the further is the assured amount available from the average. As we have seen, this pattern was altered in 1966. Districts with valuations around $12,600 had the lowest assured expenditures, but even their effective gross allowance was more than 20% higher than the statutory gross allowance. The effective gross allowance increased with movement in either direction from the $12,600 valuation although it increased at a faster rate for movement to the right of $12,600 (as valuation increased) than it did for movement to the left (reflecting a slope of 4.4 as opposed to one of 2.2).

Variation in the gross allowance is not in itself objectionable. Equal expenditures may not imply equal educational opportunity. For example, higher salaries may be necessary in order to attract a teacher of a given quality to a disadvantaged area. In this sense, Program B of 1966 can be regarded as a step in the right direction, although basing the increase on per pupil property valuation (especially when the tax base includes industrial property) is likely to be a very crude approximation of a disadvantaged area. Nonetheless, the effects of Program B can still be regarded as more desirable than the outcome if only Program A had been operative. Since the Michigan program provided a higher gross allowance than was implied by the statutory gross allowance, and for a few districts an amount close to the average, the program has been more effective as a foundation program than was adjudged earlier. But the amount assured to all but the highest valuation districts is still considerably less than the minimum equalization level. In addition, the positive relationship between the effective gross allowance and property valuation is contrary to the rationale of a foundation program, as well as to general notions of equity.

The Local Fair Share

Although our main concern in evaluating the Michigan program as a foundation program is the level of equalization established by the foundation program; a second concern is with the local share associated with the program. As already noted, the Strayer and Haig formulation uses the tax rate required for financing the entire program in the richest (highest valuation) districts as the rate to be used in calculating the local fair share.

In terms of the deductible millage (the millage used in the distribution formula), it is clear that the millage rate does not conform to the Strayer and Haig criterion. Even in 1966, when state aid became zero at a lower valuation than it had previously, the district with the highest valuation still received state aid.

If, however, the mandated millage (the millage required for full participation) had been used in the distribution formula, the millage rate would have conformed to the Strayer and Haig criterion. With a gross allowance of $255 and a deductible millage of 9 mills, for example, state aid becomes zero at a valuation of $28,333. Under these circumstances the top three percent of the K-12 districts (accounting for approximately four percent of the pupils) would have financed their foundation programs entirely from local funds.[29] With the combination of $236.50 and 8 mills (the gross allowance and mandated millage existing as of 1965), the top two percent of the K-12 districts would have financed the entire program.[30] On the basis of 1966 data, the top two to three percent of the districts would have financed their foundation programs entirely from local funds during the preceding years of the current program, had the mandated millage been used in the distribution formula.[31]

Since the deductible millage is the relevant figure with

respect to the distribution of state aid, we can conclude that the Michigan program has not been in accord with the Strayer and Haig formulation of a local fair share. Some of the implications of distributing state aid on the basis of low millage rates are considered in the next chapter.

CONCLUSIONS

The current Michigan program, a term applied to state aid expenditures on education since fiscal 1960, is composed of two main parts: a foundation program, and a variety of special grants. Aside from briefly describing the special grants, Chapter 3 is concerned with the foundation program portion of state aid.

There are three main components of the Michigan program: the gross allowance, the deductible millage, and the mandated millage. The amount of state aid which a district receives is a function of the gross allowance, the deductible millage, and the district's property valuation. During the period 1960-1966, the gross allowance (which establishes the level of the foundation program) increased from $205 per pupil to $255 per pupil. The deductible millage (which establishes the progressivity of the distribution of state aid) increased from 3.25 mills to 4.6 mills. Thus both the level of the program and the progressivity of the distribution have increased over time. In 1966, an alternate foundation program was made available to low valuation districts (districts with a per pupil SEV of less than $12,600) which, when account is taken of the ceiling in expenditures, provided a gross allowance of $338.30 with a deductible millage of 11.2 mills.

If the primary objective of the program is the avoidance of unacceptable differences in educational opportunity and that minimum acceptability involves equalization relative to average expenditures, the statutory gross allowance does not meet this objective. In 1962, the gross allowance represented

55% of average expenditures; in 1966, 57%. (The alternate foundation program, however, represented 76% of average expenditures.) In addition, the local fair share, as reflected in the deductible millage, does not conform to the Strayer and Haig criterion. (According to Strayer and Haig, the deductible millage should be the rate which would be sufficient to finance the entire program in the richest districts.)

The amount assured available to a participating district, however, is the statutory gross allowance only for a district with zero property. For all others, it is the amount raised by the mandated millage (the millage required for full participation) plus the amount of state aid. The latter is referred to as the effective gross allowance. As long as the mandated millage is greater than the deductible millage (which, except for the alternate program in 1966, was the case) the effective gross allowance increases as the district's property valuation increases. The deductible-mandated millage discrepancy means that the assured level of expenditures approaches the average for the highest valuation districts, and in that sense the Michigan program can be considered more effective than it was relative to the statutory gross allowance. The program does not, however, accomplish the objective of a foundation program for all other districts. In addition, the positive relationship between the effective gross allowance and the district's property valuation is contrary to the rationale of a foundation program, as well as to general notions of equity.

It is of interest to note that, had the mandated millage been used in the distribution formula, the resulting local fair share would have conformed to the Strayer and Haig criterion of having the share such that the highest valuation districts finance the program with local funds.

NOTES TO CHAPTER 3

1. A more complete evaluation of the current program would need to include an evaluation of the financing of state expenditures on education. In Michigan, this would mean an evaluation of the entire state system of taxation. The latter is beyond the scope of the present study. However, a few evaluations of the state's system of taxation have already been made. See, for example, Brazer (1961a). For a brief evaluation of state taxation written after the 1967 tax reform and with special reference to state expenditures on education, see Barlow (1967): IV-6 to IV-9.

2. Tableman (1951; and Sly et al. (1953): Chapter 4.

3. These three parts represented the mandatory appropriation by the state to the local school districts. Michigan, State of [4a] : X, s 23. The Primary School Interest Fund received the revenue from seven specific taxes: a special state property tax on railroad companies, telephone and telegraph companies, car loading companies and express companies, the inheritance tax, out of state insurance company taxes, and corporation organization fees.

4. Michigan, State of [10] : 269.

5. Michigan, State of [11] : 312.

6. Michigan, State of [12] : 1. Prior to 1958, the basic grant had been reduced proportionally if the earmarked funds were insufficient to finance the school aid program plus any other charges on the fund. Citizens Research Council (1962) and (1967).

7. Michigan, State of [13] : 267, s 1.

8. Two cents on every dollar subject to the sales tax are still being earmarked for school aid but now this represents one-half of a four percent sales tax whereas previously it represented two-thirds of a three percent sales tax. Michigan, State of [4b] : Article IX, s 11.

9. The $400 million represents the figure shown as the state's share of equalization plus the additional aid for low valuation. The latter is an optional foundation program available only to low valuation districts.

10. Michigan, State of [13]: 267, 15; and Michigan, State of [14]: 221, 15. One should note the inconsistency in the mere existence of hardship aid in conjunction with a foundation program. The foundation program is supposed to equalize to an acceptable level. The existence of special aid to low valuation districts (not designed to supplement the "culturally deprived" since a special grant for that purpose was established in 1966) implies that this was not, in fact, being done.

11. The reduction in valuation equals three-eights of the percentage over 125%. Michigan, State of [16]: 189, s 17.

12. Michigan, State of [15]: 222, s 1. (Tuition for special education is excluded from the ceiling.)

13. The provisions regarding tuition and transportation allowances have changed several times during the period 1960-1966. For the specific provisions pertaining to any one year, see Michigan, State of [6]; and Michigan, State of [7].

14. *Ibid.*

15. Michigan, State of [16]: 343, s 622.

16. Michigan, State of [4b]: Article IX, s 24.

17. Michigan, State of [6]: 178-193; and Michigan, State of [7]: 633.

18. State-equalized valuation rather than assessed valuation was made applicable to the distribution of state aid as a result of the Pittsfield case of 1954. (Michigan, State of [9])

State-equalized valuation represents an attempt to remove differences in the ratio of assessed valuation to market value occurring among governmental units. Equalization occurs first at the county level, at which time the percentage share of the total county valuation is established for each township and city. The same procedure then occurs at the county level where state-equalized valuation is determined for each county. The state-equalized valuation for each assessing unit (i.e., the city or township) is therefore determined by its share of the county total and by its county's share of the state total. The procedure is somewhat more complicated for school districts, since they tend to be in more than one assessing unit. For a brief evaluation of the equalization process and the application of equalization to school districts, see Cline and Taylor (1966): 22-26.

19. For the moment we will be ignoring part B of the 1966 program.

20. The term "progressive" is being used loosely in the present context. A tax is termed progressive if the tax liability as a percentage of income increases as income increases. A direct application of this definition would mean that if state aid as a percentage of SEV declines as SEV increases, expenditures are regressive. However, we are referring to expenditures rather than taxation. We will therefore invert the definition and say that if state aid as a percentage of SEV declines as SEV increases, expenditures are progressive. This was true for any year. Saying that the increase in the deductible millage resulted in a more progressive distribution implies that the ratio declined at a faster rate in 1966, for example, than it did in 1960.

21. While only about 50% of the school districts in 1966 were K-12 districts, they accounted for more than 97% of public school pupils. (Based on data from Michigan, State of [2].) These reports are available at the State Department of Education in Lansing, Michigan.

22. *Ibid.*

23. State Department of Education, oral communication.

24. In terms of the allocative efficiency criterion developed in Chapter 1, the community's local fair share would depend on the intracommunity benefit spillovers plus the private benefits from primary and secondary education.

25. In considering the existing local fair share, we will be ignoring two preliminary questions. First, is the state equalization process accurate? Second, is the existing property tax an appropriate tax base? A negative answer to either question would imply that the local fair share must be unfair. For a critical evaluation of the present system on both counts, see Barlow (1967): Chapters 3 and 4, pages 9-11.

26. Michigan, State of [3]. These reports are available at the State Department of Education in Lansing, Michigan.

27. Based on data from Michigan, State of [2]. The two average expenditure figures are not completely comparable since the 1962 figure is based on all districts and the 1966 figure on K-12 districts. However, K-12 districts in 1966 accounted for 97% of the public school pupils. Thus the two figures are nearly comparable. The reason for using different bases is that for 1966 the average for K-12 districts was readily available, but the average for all districts was not, whereas the reverse was true for 1962.

28. Among K-12 districts in 1962, there were two with a per pupil SEV in the $1,000-$2,000 range and two with a per pupil SEV of over $40,000 (one of which was over $50,000). As of 1966 there were still two districts in the $1,000-$2,000 range, and three districts above $40,000.

29. Michigan, State of [2].

30. *Ibid.*

31. Although the number and distribution of K-12 districts was not exactly the same during the period 1960-1966, the changes were relatively minor.

ALTERNATIVE FOUNDATION PROGRAMS

In **Chapter 4**, three alternative foundation programs are briefly considered. The distribution of state aid resulting from two of the alternative programs is then compared to the distribution of state aid associated with the current program.

Our criteria for an alternative program being judged "better" are a gross allowance more likely to avoid unacceptable differences in educational opportunity, and a deductible millage which conforms to the Strayer and Haig formulation.[1] A second concern is with the cost of the alternative programs. The cost of a foundation program is:

C = gross allowance x number of pupils - deductible millage x SEV. The estimated cost of the alternative programs is based on the K-12 data for 1966.[2]

ALTERNATIVE PROGRAM A

Under the present program, state aid equals zero at a per pupil SEV of $55,435, which in Michigan means that all districts receive some state aid. One way to improve the present program would be to keep the bottom of the distribution line at its present point (state aid = 0 at a per pupil SEV of $55,435) and rotate the line upward until it intersects the vertical axis at $440.97. This is illustrated in Figure 5. Since we know state aid is zero at $55,435 and the gross allowance is $440.97, we can calculate the deductible millage. This is equal to 7.95 mills.

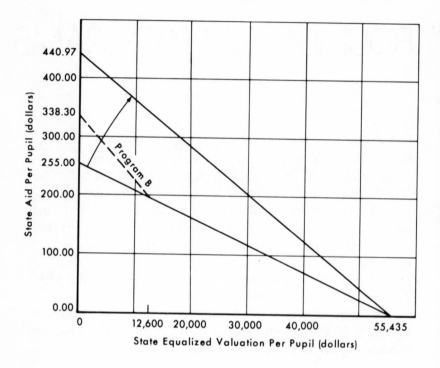

Figure 5   ALTERNATIVE FOUNDATION PROGRAM A

The resulting foundation program would provide a gross allowance equal to the average operating expenditures in 1966. This is the minimum level assumed to avoid unacceptable differences in educational opportunity. The program therefore would accomplish the primary objective of a foundation program.

Alternative A would also have considerable political appeal since no one would receive less state aid than he received in 1966 (a condition we might regard as fulfilling a politician's Pareto criterion). We can see from Figure 5 that the introduction of Program B in 1966 is in keeping with this approach. However, the cause of the discrepancy between the nominal provisions of Program B and the actual provisions reflects the major problem with this alternative, which itself is quite obvious—it is very costly. The estimated cost of the program is $635 million. This represents more than a 60% increase in the 1966 equalization expenditures.

It is obvious that if there are no limitations on the cost of the program, any program could be accomplished. Unlimited state expenditures on equalization are neither a realistic assumption nor a desirable one because of the opportunity costs involved. We therefore will regard the cost of the program as a constraining factor and assume that for political reasons this cost must approximate current expenditures on equalization.

The deductible millage also does not conform to the Strayer and Haig formulation under which the richest districts finance their foundation programs locally. This was implicit in having state aid become zero at the 1966 level, at which point all received some state aid.

ALTERNATIVE PROGRAM B

Alternative B remedies the major problem of the first program by using the actual expenditures on equalization in

1966 as the cost of the program. The number of pupils and the equalized property valuation are parameters. With the cost held constant, the only variables are the gross allowance and the deductible millage.

In Program B, the 9 mills required for participation in the program in 1966 is used to establish the local fair share. The gross allowance which can be provided under these conditions is $326. With a gross allowance of $326 and a deductible millage of 9 mills, state aid becomes zero at an SEV of $36,222, thus requiring that the top .9% of the districts finance the foundation program without state aid. This does not conflict with the Strayer and Haig criterion, but it is clearly a narrow definition of what is meant by the richest districts. However, the gross allowance is not quite 75% of the $440 we have been using as the minimum level at which to equalize.

If the $440 per pupil is to be provided while using a deductible millage of 9 mills, it would cost around $607 million. Since we are using a higher deductible millage, the cost is less than in Program A, but it still represents a 55% increase over current expenditures.

ALTERNATIVE PROGRAM C

If the 1966 mandated millage of 9 mills is to be used as the deductible millage, it will be necessary either to lower the level of the foundation program or to substantially increase expenditures on equalization (attempt to remove the assumed budget constraint) or some combination of the two. If, however, we use the average local levy as a reference point, the deductible millage which would result in a local fair share is 16.09 mills.

The 16.09 mills conforms with the criterion of using a tax rate so that the highest valuation districts are self-supporting. With a gross allowance of $440.97 and a deductible millage of 16.09, state aid becomes zero at a per pupil valuation of $27,406. For 1966 this would mean that the 14 highest valuation districts (out of the 530 K-12 districts) would not receive state aid.[3] The estimated cost of the program is $425 million, implying an 8 to 9% increase over 1966 equalizaton expenditures. This represents some violation of the assumed budget constraint. However, the increase is small enough to be regarded as an incremental change in the program and probably within the realm of political feasibility.

COMPARATIVE ANALYSIS OF STATE AID DISTRIBUTIONS

A Lorenz curve provides a useful way of looking at the existing distribution of state aid and the effects of some of the proposed changes on the distribution. A Lorenz curve shows the degree of inequality in the distribution of a variable, usually in the distribution of income. For our purposes, we plot the cumulative percentage of pupils on the vertical axis (beginning with the district with the lowest per pupil valuation and moving upward) and the cumulative percentage of state aid on the horizontal axis. When a Lorenz curve is being used, a 45° line is usually termed the line of equal distribution. Here, a 45° line shows a proportional distribution of state aid under which each district receives the same amount per pupil, irrespective of the district's valuation. Within this framework, we can regard a policy which moves the curve away from the 45° line in a southeasterly direction as increasing the progressivity of the distribution.[4]

Four Lorenz curves are shown in Figure 6 reflecting existing or alternative patterns of distribution.[5] Program 1 shows the distribution which would have resulted if only Program A of 1966—gross allowance (g.a.) = $266; deductible millage (d.m.) = 4.6—had been operative. It can be regarded as a proxy for the distribution that occured in the previous years. In fact, the distribution under A of 1966 was more

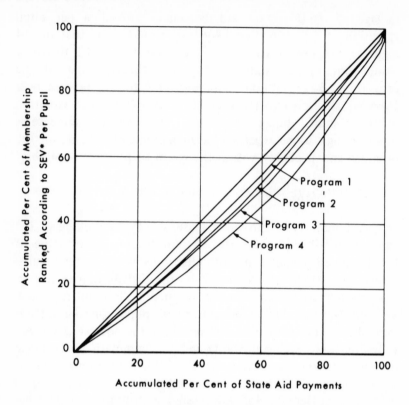

Figure 6   ALTERNATIVE PAYMENTS OF STATE AID

Program 1: Gross Allowance of $255, deductible millage of 4.6;

Program 2: As above for districts with $12,600 SEV* per pupil or
more. For others: Gross allowance of $338 and deductible
millage of 11.1. Program B state aid payments = 2/3 ((380
− 14.5 SEV) − (255 − 4.6 SEV)) + 255 − 4.6 SEV;

Program 3: Total actually spent in fiscal year 1966 (Program B), but
with deductible millage equal to qualifying millage equal to
9 mills (in this case the gross allowance is $326);

Program 4: Gross allowance of $440; deductible millage of 16.09 (re-
flecting the 1966 average operating expenditures and average local levy, respectively).

*State equalized valuation

progressive than the previous programs had been, since the deductible millage was higher than it had been previously. Program 2 is based on the actual program in 1966 (g.a. = $255, d.m. = 4.6, for districts with a per pupil SEV more than $12,600; 2/3 [(380 - .0145 SEV) - (255 - .0046 SEV)] + (255 - .0046 SEV) for districts with a per pupil SEV less than $12,600). Program 3 shows the distribution resulting from alternative Program B (g.a. = $326; d.m. = 9).[6] This is the program which would have resulted if the mandated millage had been used in the distribution formula, given the actual 1966 equalization expenditures. Program 4 shows the distribution resulting from alternative Program C (g.a. = $440.97; d.m. = 16.09). This is the program under which the gross allowance reflected the actual per pupil operating expenditures in 1966 and the deductible millage is based on the average local levy in 1966. The figures for selected points on the four Lorenz curves are shown in Table 5.[7]

From Figure 6 we can see that the distribution from Program 1—the proxy for the years prior to 1966—was only mildly progressive. This reflects the use of a low deductible millage. The lower the deductible millage, the flatter the line, and the flatter the line, the more it approximates a proportional distribution.

The introduction of the optional foundation program for low valuation districts results in curve 2's being to the right of curve 1. Curve 2's being to the right of curve 1 is also, in part, illustrative of the comment in Chapter 3 that the distribution of state aid has been becoming more progressive over time.[8] The distance between the curves increases up to the forty-fifth percentile of pupils and then begins to decline. This reflects the steeper slope (higher deductible millage) associated with the optional program and also the fact that the optional program ends at a per pupil valuation which is slightly under the mean ($12,600 as opposed to $13,700).

TABLE 5

SELECTED POINTS FROM THE LORENZ CURVES
OF FIGURE 6

Accumulated Percent of Pupils[a]	Accumulated Percent of State Aid Payments			
	Program 1	Program 2	Program 3	Program 4
	(approximate)			
2.6	3.2	3.7	3.6	4.3
5.3	6.4	7.3	7.2	8.4
16.4	19.1	21.2	21.3	24.3
24.9	28.6	31.2	31.6	35.7
49.9	55.2	57.6	59.5	65.2
70.6	74.9	76.2	78.3	82.7
90.0	92.5	92.9	94.4	97.7

a.   The accumulation was done in terms of the number of pupils and the dollars of state aid. The accumulated pupils and the corresponding accumulated payments were recorded at intervals of 50,000 pupils or as close to 50,000 as was possible without splitting districts. After the numbers were accumulated, the corresponding percentages were calculated. This is why the percentages are approximate and also why they are at slightly irregular intervals.

In terms of Figure 6, curves 2 and 3 (the actual distribution in 1966 and the distribution which would have resulted if the total expenditures had remained the same and the mandated millage had been used in the distribution formula) are indistinguishable until about the twenty-fifth percentile of students. The reason is that using a gross allowance of $338 and a deductible millage of 11.2 (the relevant foundation program for a low valuation districts) is not very different from using a gross allowance of $326 and a deductible millage of 9 for the lower low-valuation districts. In terms of the distribution formula, this is because the difference in the slope compensates for the difference in the intercept, at least for a while. From Table 5 and Appendix 1, we can see that, in fact, curve 3 lies to the left of curve 2 until the fifth percentile of pupils. After that, curve 3 is to the right of curve 2. The distance between the two curves reaches a maximum at about the sixtieth percentile of pupils and declines thereafter. What this shows is that the very lowest valuation districts (the bottom 5%) and the higher valuation districts (the top 40%) were better off with the dual program existing in 1966 than they would have been had the mandated millage been used in the distribution formula.

Curve 4, which represents the alternative program based on the 1966 averages, lies to the right of the three preceding curves. From Appendix 1 it can be seen that the point at which the distance between curves 3 and 4 is greatest is at the fifty-third percentile of pupils. In other words, the top 47% would be better off under the alternative program based on the mandated millage than under the alternative based on the 1966 averages. Of more interest is the comparison between the actual 1966 program and the first alternative, curves 2 and 4. Again from Appendix 1, it can be seen that the distance between the two curves is greatest at the fifty-seventh percentile. This means that the top 43% were better off with the actual 1966 program than they would be with the alternative based on the averages.

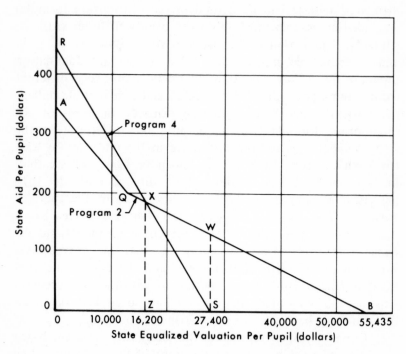

Figure 7   DISTRIBUTION OF STATE AID: PROGRAMS 2 AND 4

The relationship between what is shown in the Lorenz curves and the earlier diagrams used to describe the distribution of state aid can be seen from Figure 7. RS shows the distribution which results from Program 4; AQB, the distribution from Program 2. The point at which the distance between the two Lorenz curves is greatest occurs at X, the point where RS intersects AQB. The 43% who would be worse off correspond to the students whose districts' per pupil valuations are greater than $16,200. The districts which would be worse off are those between Z and B. However, we know that only 3% of the districts (and 4% of the students) are represented by the line SB.[9] The relevant portion of ZB is therefore ZS, that is, the districts with a per pupil valuation between $16,200 and $27,400. The reduction in state aid for these districts is shown by XSW. The districts which would gain by the adoption of Program 4 are those with a per pupil valuation less than $16,200. Their gain is shown by the tetragon RAQX.

IMPLICATIONS AND CONCLUSIONS

In Chapter 3, we concluded that the Michigan program has been deficient as a foundation program. The basic reason is that the equalization has not been at the minimum level assumed necessary for avoiding unacceptable differences in educational opportunity. Two likely reasons for this are that state equalization expenditures have been insufficient and/or the distribution has been inappropriate. From the discussion on the alternative programs, it appears to be a little of both, but mostly a matter of distribution.

Under the unit grant foundation program, distribution is determined by the deductible millage. The use of low deductible millage rates has meant that the distribution has not differed greatly from a flat per pupil grant. Given the likelihood of a budget constraint, this can be expected to result in a low gross allowance. Thus the use of too low a deductible millage not only means aid goes to the wealthy districts, but is likely to mean that there will be large discrepancies in the level of educational services provided.

We have also seen that with a small increase in expenditures it would be possible to establish a program which is generally consistent with the objectives of a foundation program. This is the program discussed as alternative Program C, which provided for a gross allowance of $440.97 and a deductible millage of 16.09 mills. The $440 represents the average per pupil expenditures, the minimum figure assumed to avoid unacceptable differences in educational opportunity.[10] The use of a deductible millage of 16.09 mills conforms to the Strayer and Haig criterion of setting the deductible millage at the rate needed to finance the program in the richest districts. In view of this, the program is quite moderate.

There is still one major or potential problem with the suggested program. The program is set up to provide (1966) average operating expenditures for all participating districts. The problem involves the possibility that some districts may not participate when the required millage is, say, 16.09 mills. To the extent that districts do not participate, the objective of equalizing at a certain level of expenditures will not be accomplished. One way of alleviating the problem would be to make it compulsory that all districts levy no less than the deductible millage. A possible justification for making the deductible millage compulsory would be that children are already forced to attend school and that the state is now attempting to make the forced attendance meaningful. This approach is objectionable for several reasons. A compulsory millage rate would violate one of the other stated objectives of the Michigan program—that of local control. Not allowing district residents the opportunity of allocating their resources according to their own preferences is contrary to any achievement of allocative efficiency.[11] Perhaps the major reason, however, is that it is an unnecessarily crude way of achieving the general objectives of the program. In any case, the introduction of a compulsory deductible millage can be considered to be politically infeasible.

In the presence of both a budget constraint and a non-compulsory deductible millage, it will probably be necessary to make some trade-off between the use of a high gross allowance-high deductible millage and a low gross allowance-low deductible millage. The use of a deductible millage which is high enough to provide equalization at an "acceptable" level in the presence of a budget constraint is likely to mean that some districts cannot or will not participate. The possibility of nonparticipation can be minimized through the use of a lower deductible millage. For example, in 1966, the first year after the 1 mill increase in the mandated millage, 8% of the K-12 districts, accounting for only 3% of the pupils, levied less than the required 9 mills. But we have also seen that in terms of 1966 equalization expenditures the use of a 9 mill deductible millage implies a gross allowance of only $326. Thus either choice is likely to result in some sacrifice in the achievement of the program's objectives.

Previously it was noted that equalization, particularly as it exists in a foundation program, might be incompatible with other expressed objectives of the Michigan program. It now appears that the primary objective of the foundation program —avoiding socially and politically unacceptable differences in the level of educational services made available—may be incompatible with its own structure. Further analysis of either type of incompatibility requires our considering the effects of state aid on local district expenditures.

NOTES TO CHAPTER 4

1. Strayer and Haig (1924): 204. In discussing alternative programs, the proposed deductible millage figure also serves as the mandated millage.

2. The basic source of the data is the Michigan, State of [2]. Much of this information, including all of the information needed to make the calculations in the following sections, has been stored on tape by the State Department of Education. A reproduction of the data was provided by John Forsythe of the Michigan School Finance Study.

3. In this case, the deductible millage would be set by the rate needed to finance the program for the top three percent of the districts, which accounted for about four percent of the students.

4. This is analogous to calling a tax policy progressive if it moves the Lorenz curve reflecting the distribution of income closer toward the $45°$ line. (In this case, the cumulative percentage of income recipients is plotted on one axis, the cumulative percentage of income on the other.) See Musgrave (1959): 224-225.

5. The data used to plot the curves are given in Appendix 1.

6. We have not shown the distribution resulting from "alternative Program A" because in this case the total expenditures were more than $245 million above the actual expenditures in 1966. A comparison of the Lorenz curves resulting from different distributions is meaningful only if the total being distributed remains at least approximately the same. The total expenditures resulting from Programs 1 through 4 in Figure 6 are not exactly the same. The expenditure from Programs 1 and 4 differs from those under Programs 2 and 3 by approximately -$22 million and +$35 million, respectively.

7. For more detail, see Appendix 1.

8. However, the increase in the progressivity of the distribution is understated by the distance between curves 1 and 2, since curve 1 overstates the progressivity of the distribution of state aid in the early 1960's.

9. See Chapter 4, footnote 3, above.

10. Additional assistance could be made to districts in which the cost of the inputs which enter the educational process is unusually high.

11. It should be noted that compulsory attendance is also contrary to allocative efficiency.

THE EFFECTS OF STATE AID ON EDUCATIONAL EXPENDITURES

Thus far our evaluation of state aid for primary and secondary schools in Michigan has remained entirely within the structural framework of a foundation program. We have, moreover, based the evaluation only on the criteria appropriate to the objectives of a foundation program. In Chapter 4, however, we concluded that a workable foundation program could not be formulated without considering the effects of state aid on the local district's expenditure decisions. This is the subject of Chapter 5. We shall rely on basic demand theory in analyzing the effects of the current program. First, the underlying theoretical framework is developed. Then, in view of this framework and some of the available data on local district expenditures, we shall estimate the effects of state aid on educational expenditures. Proceeding in this manner serves several purposes. It enables us to evaluate further the effects of the current program. In the process, it allows us to evaluate the foundation program approach as a method of distributing state aid. Finally, it provides us with a basis for formulating alternative programs of aid, given various objectives, and priorities among these objectives. The evaluation of the foundation program and the formulation of alternative programs is the subject of Chapter 6.

Throughout this chapter the state aid program is considered from the point of view of the local district. Our main concern is with the change in the district's preferred position

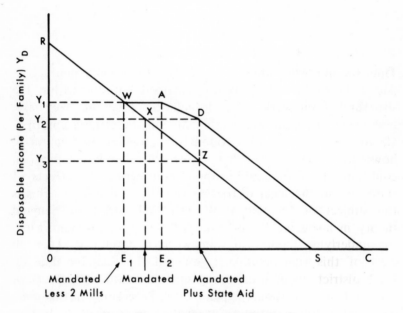

Figure 8   THE EFFECT OF THE MICHIGAN FOUNDATION
             PROGRAM ON A DISTRICT'S OPPORTUNITY LINE

which is likely to result from the current program.[1] The district's decisions regarding educational expenditures are expected to be affected by factors other than state aid, but for present purposes these other factors are assumed to be held constant.[2]

THE EFFECTS OF STATE AID

We can view state aid as affecting the district's opportunity line. This is shown in Figure 8. Disposable income (per family) is plotted on the vertical axis, expenditures on education (per pupil) on the horizontal axis.[3] The line RS indicates the district's opportunity line in the absence of state aid; RWAC, the opportunity line with state aid. Both the distance of RS from the origin and the size of SC varies among districts. The relationship between RS and SC (the amount of state aid) is not the same for all districts, since state aid is a function of property valuation rather than income.[4] The RW portion of the line is unaffected by state aid, since no state aid is received if the local levy is more than 2 mills below the mandated millage of 8 mills (9 in 1966). Once the minimum is levied, the district's opportunity line shifts from W to A. In other words, a 6 mill levy (7 as of 1966) no longer produces 6 mills' worth of education (E_1) but 6 mills' worth plus the additional amount of education made available from six-eights of the district's state aid (E_2). Increasing the local levy to the mandated level is associated with proportional increases in state aid. Increasing the local levy beyond the mandated level is not associated with additional amounts of state aid (i.e., XD = SC).[5]

While Figure 8 shows the after-state-aid opportunity line associated with any given level of expenditures from local resources, our concern is with the way state aid is likely to affect the district's expenditure decisions. This will depend in large part on the type of grant the district is being offered. The current program contains three types of grants:

(a) a matching grant
(b) a matching grant subject to a minimum local contribution
(c) a lump-sum grant

Which grant is relevant depends on the district's "initial position," the district's expenditures in the absence of the state aid program. We proceed by considering each of the grants separately.[6] Having examined how a district can be expected to react to various kinds of grants, we can refer back to Figure 8 and consider the "if–then" issue which is our main concern. In other words, if the district is within a certain range on its initial opportunity line, then it is likely to end up within a certain range on its after-state-aid opportunity line. Given this, the available data on income, state aid, and educational expenditures by school district, and one additional assumption, we can estimate the impact of the current program on educational expenditures. For convenience, we establish the following notation:

E_1 = the district's initial expenditures on education; i.e., expenditures in the absence of state aid (unobservable)

E_2 = the district's total expenditures with state aid (observable)

L = the district's "local levy," representing the expenditures from local resources associated with a given E_2 (observable)

By definition (as well as by law) $E_2 - L$ = state aid at any time.

MATCHING GRANT

Under the current program, a matching grant exists only for a very small range of the district's expenditures on education. However, it is easier to see the effects of this part of the program if we assume that state aid is given on a matching basis for all ranges of expenditures. We also assume that the matching grant is in some constant proportion to the district's expenditures on education.

An example of a matching grant is shown in Figure 9. As before, disposable income is on the vertical axis, expenditures on education on the horizontal axis, RS is the district's initial opportunity line, and RC the opportunity line with state aid. At any given point, the horizontal distance between the two opportunity lines equals the amount of state aid at that point. This means that for any location on RC we can move back horizontally to RS to find the district's expenditures from local resources (the observable local levy) associated with that level of total expenditures.

Effects of a Matching Grant

The district's initial position is at W, where it is spending OE_1 on education and spending OY_1 on other goods. Distributing state aid as a matching grant is analogous to a reduction in the price of education, and we can view the expected results in terms of the standard analysis of a reduction in price.[7] This means we can view a matching grant as having a substitution effect and an income effect, both of which will lead to an increase in expenditures on education as long as education is not an inferior good.

The substitution effect is separated from the income effect in order to isolate the effect solely due to the change

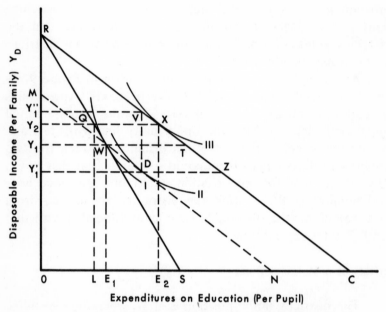

Figure 9   THE POTENTIAL RESULTS OF A MATCHING GRANT ON
DISPOSABLE INCOME AND EXPENDITURES ON EDUCATION

in relative prices. This is done by holding real income "constant." Within the Slutsky approach, which is the one used here, real income is constant if the consumer is just able to buy the old bundle of goods, given the change in price. The substitution effect may therefore be shown by drawing a line MN parallel to RC through point W. Since the slope of RC (the price or opportunity line with state aid) is flatter than RS, MN parallel to RC is also flatter than RS. If we invoke the usual assumption of convex indifference curves,[8] this must move the preferred position to the right of W, which in Figure 9 is shown at D. In other words, a reduction in the price of education relative to other goods leads to an increase in the amount being spent on education, all other things being equal. If we now take account of the income effect (the shift upward from MN to RC) we can see that the district will end up somewhere between points V and Z as long as its income elasticity[9] of demand for education is positive. (The possibility of a negative income elasticity with respect to education is assumed irrelevant.) The district's preferred position is shown as being at X, where total expenditures on education equal OE_2 and expenditures on other goods equal OY_2.

Expected outcome: Since distributing state aid as a matching grant in effect lowers the price of education relative to all other goods, we can expect that in the absence of an upward sloping demand curve there will be an increase in total expenditures on education. As in the case of any other price reduction, a matching grant also results in an increase in the district's income. Unless the income elasticity for education is very high, we can expect a portion of the increase in income to be used in increasing expenditure on other goods. In other words, some of the grant is taken as an increase in the district's disposable income. This occurs even though the amount of the grant is dependent on the district's expenditures on education, and state aid can be used only for education. Thus, in our example, the district's preferred position is shown to be at X. While total expenditures have increased at X (from OE_1 to OE_2), expenditures from local resources have declined (from OE_1 to OL). This implies that Y_1Y_2 is taken as an increase in disposable income.

Other possible outcomes: Although we expect some of the grant to be used in freeing local resources, it is possible that the district could end up devoting the same amount of its own resources to education. This would correspond to being at T. It is also possible the district could end up increasing its expenditures from local resources, that is, end up between T and Z.[10] While the latter two are possibilities, we will consider them unlikely because of the very high income elasticities which are implied.

Estimating the District's Initial Position

In general, we expect the district's total expenditures to be greater than its initial expenditures but less than its initial expenditures plus state aid. In terms of Figure 9, we expect the district's position on RC (total expenditures) to be above and to the right of its initial position. How much above and how much to the right depends on the degree of change in relative prices and on the district's income elasticity for education (or, in other words, on the district's price elasticity of demand for education).

Since the difference between total expenditures and expenditures from local resources at any time is equal to the amount of state aid, we may estimate the district's initial point either from its observed total expenditures (as above) or its observed local levy. Thus, we expect the district's observed total expenditures, such as OE_2, to be to the right of OE_1. Alternatively, we expect the district's observed local levy, such as OL, to be to the left of OE_1.

MATCHING GRANT SUBJECT TO A MINIMUM LOCAL CONTRIBUTION

The first part of the current program can be used as an example of a matching grant requiring a minimum local contribution. In other words, we assume that state aid is given as a matching grant on the condition that the district levies, say, 6 mills worth of expenditures.

In Figure 10 and Figure 11, the amount of local expenditures required for participation is equal to OL and OL_1 respectively. RS shows the districts's initial opportunity line, RZMC the after-state-aid opportunity line. Alternatively, given a point on MC, we can regard that point as showing total expenditures and the corresponding point on RS expenditures from local resources.

The district's initial position is at W, where it is spending OE_1 on education and OY_1 on other goods. If the matching grant had been unrestricted, as in the previous example (that is, if the dashed line RM had been a relevant possibility), the district would have chosen X. The resulting expenditure position has not been marked, but as before total expenditures would have increased, although expenditures from local resources would have declined, relative to the E_1 position. The requirement for receiving the grant, however, precludes this possibility.

Effects of Requiring a Minimum Local Contribution

Requiring a minimum local contribution for the receipt of state aid produces a kink in the district's (potential) price line. Normally the "price reduction" associated with a matching grant can be described as a pivoting of the price line. While MC represents the bottom portion of a pivoted line, the change occurring at M is a shift rather than a pivot—or, in other words, a kink. This in turn accentuates the change in

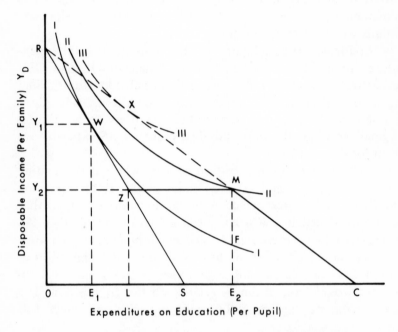

Figure 10   THE POTENTIAL RESULTS OF A MATCHING GRANT
SUBJECT TO A MINIMUM LOCAL CONTRIBUTION: CASE A

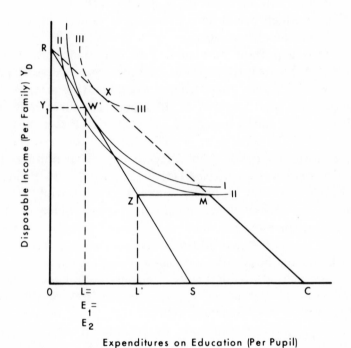

Expenditures on Education (Per Pupil)

Figure 11   THE POTENTIAL RESULTS OF A MATCHING GRANT
SUBJECT TO A MINIMUM LOCAL CONTRIBUTION: CASE B

the price line occurring at M. Any district which is initially
above Z is thus offered a strong inducement to move to M, an
inducement which will be accepted as long as being at M
places the district in a position preferred to its initial position.
The inducement to move to M is, of course, relevant only to
a district which would have ended up at some point on RM if
it had been able to do so.

Two important outcomes: Two important outcomes are
shown in Figures 10 and 11. In both cases, curve II passes
through the corner of the altered price line (the after-state-aid
opportunity line) at point M. In Figure 10, curve II is above
curve I (the initial position). The district therefore prefers
being at M rather than at W. The district's total expenditures
on education increase from OE_1 to OE_2. Expenditures from
local resources also increase—from OE_1 to OL. In Figure 11,
however, curve II is below curve I. The district therefore
prefers to remain at W, its initial position. Since at W the
district is spending less than the required amount for participation, the initial expenditures, the observable total expenditures, and the observable local levy are all the same.

We can see from Figure 10 that requiring a minimum
local contribution can be a very effective way of stimulating
expenditures on education (stimulation being defined as an
increase in total expenditures by an amount which is greater
than the amount of state aid; i.e., $E_2 - E_1 > E_2 - L$). As
noted previously, this can happen with a regular matching
grant, but it is not very likely. The reason is that the income
effect associated with a matching grant (our equivalent to a
price reduction in education) usually leads to an increase in
the amount taken as disposable income, as well as to an
increase in expenditures on education. With the use of a
required minimum, the district's choices have been restricted
to remaining at a point such as W or moving to M. While the
latter results in an increase in the district's real income (by an
amount MF), there is not an income effect associated with

the movement, at least not in the usual sense of the term.[11] Instead, we might label this a displacement effect. The same reason which makes this an effective way of increasing expenditures on education also means that the district ends up at a worse position than it would with an unrestricted choice of positions.

Other possible outcomes: Remaining at the initial position or going to the point corresponding to the minimum requirement are not the only two possibilities under a matching grant subject to a minimum local contribution. One obvious possibility is that the required minimum is to the left of the district's initial position. In particular, the required minimum may be enough to the left of E_1 for the district to reach a point such as X, its preferred position under the matching scheme. In this case, the minimum is irrelevant.

Estimating the Initial Position

The use of a minimum requirement with a matching grant thereafter makes it difficult to estimate the district's initial position. At first glance, it might appear that we could at least say that a district which is observed spending the minimum local contribution plus the aid associated with that level must have initially been spending less than the required minimum. This may be the case, but not necessarily. Discussion of the latter possibility is postponed until we consider the expected effects of the current program as a whole. If the district is a nonparticipant, the initial and observable positions are the same and estimation is not a problem.

LUMP-SUM GRANT WITH AN IRRELEVANT MINIMUM

We can use an abbreviated form of the current program as the basis for our example of a lump-sum grant. We assume: (1) there is a minimum requirement for receiving the grant;

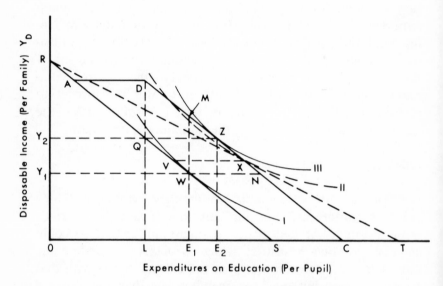

Figure 12 THE POTENTIAL RESULTS OF A MATCHING GRANT
WITH AN IRRELEVANT MINIMUM

(2) the district receives a fixed amount as long as it levies at least the required amount; and (3) the required minimum is irrelevant (it is less than the district's initial expenditures). This is shown in Figure 12. The same format is being used so that RS depicts the district's initial opportunity line and RS also corresponds to expenditures from local resources, and so forth.

Effects of a Lump-Sum Grant

The district's initial position is at W, where it is spending OE_1 on education and OY_1 on other goods. As long as the district's expenditures from local resources are at least equal to those at A, the district receives state aid equal to AD. Since the amount of state aid is fixed for any district, AD equals SC and DC (the after-state-aid opportunity line) is parallel to RS (the district's initial opportunity line). DC parallel to RS indicates that relative prices have remained the same and the effect of the grant depends on the district's income elasticity for education.

Expected outcome: We have already assumed that neither education nor all other goods (disposable income) is an inferior good. We can therefore expect both total expenditures on education and expenditures on other goods to increase. In terms of Figure 12, we expect the district to be somewhere between M and N. Where depends on its income elasticity for education. In Figure 12, it is assumed that the district's income elasticity is such that it chooses to go to Z. In this case, the district's total expenditures on education increase from OE_1 to OE_2 and its expenditures from local resources decline from OE_1 to OL. In other words, Y_1Y_2 is taken as an increase in disposable income.

The effect of a lump-sum grant depends only on the district's income elasticity, because a lump-sum grant is equivalent to an increase in the district's income by an amount equal to the grant. This occurs even though the grant itself can only be spent on education. We can see this if we suppose that the district's income increases by an amount equal to SC. The increase could either be due to an increase in family income or to the receipt of an untied grant. In this case, the line DC would extend back to the vertical axis (as it would with a lump-sum grant if we had not included an irrelevant minimum). Assuming neither is an inferior good, the district could spend WM on other goods or WN on education. Since it is the same district with the same change in its opportunity line, the district again chooses to go to Z, where it is spending OY_2 on other goods and OE_2 on education, which is the conclusion reached above. In other words, a lump-sum grant given ostensibly for some particular function is, in effect, an untied grant.

In the discussion of an effective required minimum, we considered the possibility of stimulating expenditures on education, defining the latter as $E_2 - E_1 > E_2 - L$. Another way of saying this is that expenditures from local resources increase relative to the E_1 position (at which point all expenditures are from local resources). From Figure 12 we can see that this is an irrelevant possibility under a lump-sum grant. At most, the district could spend the entire amount of the grant on education, which implies being at N with expenditures from local resources at W. In this case, initial expenditures would equal expenditures from local resources (OL = OE_1). However, this too is an unreasonable outcome, since it implies that the income elasticity for all other goods is zero.

Lump-Sum Grant Versus a Matching Grant

Figure 12 also allows us to compare the effects of giving the same district an equal amount of state aid by means of a matching grant as opposed to a lump-sum grant. In order to make the comparison, we need a change in the price line which gives the district the same amount of state aid it has at Z. In other words, state aid must equal QZ (= AD = SC). The required change in the price line is found by rotating RS rightward from point R until a point is found which both is on DC and represents a tangency between the rotated price line and an indifference curve. Continuing the assumption of a convex indifference curve implies that the point of tangency must be below and to the right of Z. In Figure 12, the price line which fulfills these conditions is the dashed line RT, intersecting DC at X. State aid is equal to VX which is equal to QZ. At X total expenditures on education have increased and expenditures on other goods have declined relative to Z.

Thus, for a given amount of aid we can expect the increase in expenditures on education to be greater under a matching grant than under a lump-sum grant. The reason is that the matching grant changes relative prices in favor of education and therefore encourages the district to increase its expenditures on education relative to expenditures on all other goods. The lump-sum grant, however, only increases the district's income. It does not change relative prices. From the district's point of view, the lump-sum grant is better than a matching grant, since a lump-sum grant allows the district to reach a more preferred position relative to its own preferences.

Estimating the Initial Position

Under the lump-sum grant we can expect the district's observed total expenditures on education to be greater than the district's initial expenditures, but by an amount which is less than the amount of state aid. Alternatively, we can expect the observed local levy to be less than the initial expenditures. How much of the aid given as a lump-sum grant will be spent on education (i.e., how much L is to the left of

E_1 or how much E_2 is to the right of E_1) will depend on the district's income elasticity for education.

The Ceiling Effect of the Required Minimum

The expected effect of the lump-sum grant becomes more complicated if the district's initial position is between A (the expenditures from local resources required to receive the aid) and Q (the expenditures from local resources which correspond to the required amount plus the amount of state aid received).[12] If the district is close to Q or if its income elasticity is very high, the expected results are the same as before. The closer the district is to A, and especially if its income elasticity is relatively low, the less option it has regarding the use of the grant. What is happening is that the irrelevant minimum local contribution is again beginning to have an effect, although the effect is different from the one discussed in an earlier section. In this case, the required minimum acts as a ceiling on the amount of the grant which the district can take as disposable income. This, in turn, implies that the proportion of the grant being used for education increases as the district's initial position approaches A. The limiting case of the ceiling occurs for a district which is initially at A, in which case it ends up at D. For a district initially at A, total expenditures on education therefore increase by the full amount of the grant.

EXPECTED EFFECTS OF THE CURRENT PROGRAM

Thus far we have considered the expected effects of each of three types of grants. The current program is a combination of a minimum requirement grant, a matching grant, and a lump-sum grant. The expected effects of having these three components in one grant program is somewhat different from the expected effects of any one of the grants or of a combination of any two of the components. We therefore need to consider how a district can be expected to react to a program which is a combination of these three grants, the "if–then" issue mentioned at the beginning of the chapter. This, in turn, allows us to consider the implied initial positions of the districts, given what we know about their observable positions.

In order to view the potential change in the district's opportunity line associated with the current program, we again need Figure 8. To facilitate the discussion, Figure 8 is reproduced as Figure 13.

The "If–Then" Issue

For a district which is initially spending more than two mills below the mandated amount, which corresponds to being between R and W, the current program appears as a matching grant with a required minimum. In this case, we can expect that the district either remains where it is or goes to A, where total expenditures equal 2 mills below the mandated plus the amount of state aid associated with that point. A district which by chance is initially spending 2 mills below the mandated level and is therefore at W can also be expected to go to A rather than remain at W. We can assume that the same amount of income with more education is preferable to the same income with less education. Or, in other words, when the price of an additional amount of education is zero, we can expect the district to take whatever is being offered.

A district which is initially spending between 2 mills below the mandated level and the mandated millage, which corresponds to being between W and X, is also likely to go to A. A district initially between W and X faces a matching grant with a required minimum where the required minimum serves as a ceiling. As the discussion in the preceding section has shown, the level of total expenditures which corresponds to a

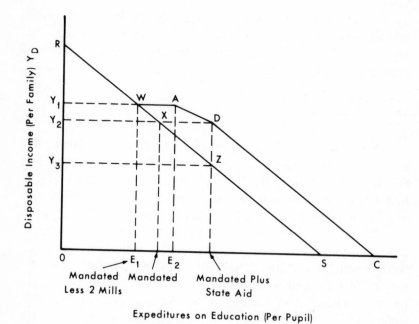

Figure 13   THE POTENTIAL RESULTS OF THE MICHIGAN FOUNDATION PROGRAM
ON DISPOSABLE INCOME AND EXPENDITURES ON EDUCATION

minimum requirement (in this case the minimum equals 2 mills below the mandated) restricts the options of a district which is initially just beyond the minimum. The closer the district is to the mandated level (that is, the closer it is to X) and the higher its income elasticity, the less relevant is the ceiling effect associated with the minimum.

For a district initially spending between the mandated amount and the mandated amount plus state aid, which corresponds to being between X and Z, the relevant part of the program is likely to be the matching program. In general, we can expect the district to move in a northeasterly direction and therefore end up between A and D (at D, total expenditures are equal to the mandated amount plus state aid).

For a district initially spending at least the mandated expenditures plus state aid, which corresponds to be at Z or between Z and S, state aid appears as a lump-sum (or untied) grant. We can expect a district in this position to end up somewhere beyond D. How much beyond D depends on the district's initial position and on its income elasticity for education.

Implications

It is very difficult to estimate a district's initial position if its observable position is either at A or D, which corresponds to an observable local levy of 2 mills less than the mandated and the mandated, respectively. The reason is that both A and D, but especially A, are "corner points." As such, they become possible preferred positions for districts which initially may have been in very different positions.

Fortunately for purposes of estimation, there have been very few districts to the left of D (corresponding to an observable local levy less than the mandated). We can expect that any district which is at D would, in the absence of state aid, have spent no less than the mandated amount. If the district was at X and chose to go to D, it would imply that it was reacting to the lump-sum grant and chose to spend all of its additional income on education. As noted previously, this is unreasonable, since it implies a zero income elasticity for everything else. This means that any district which has an observable local levy equal to the mandated (the local levy which corresponds to a total expenditure of D) would, in the absence of state aid, be spending something between the mandated portion and the mandated portion plus state aid.[13] What is more relevant is that districts which are beyond D (and therefore have an observable local levy greater than the mandated) are responding to a lump-sum grant.

We already know that, as of 1966, for example, the average local levy was slightly more than 16 mills, which is 180% of the mandated amount. We also know that only 8% of the K-12 districts (representing only 3% of the pupils) had a local levy equal to or less than the mandated levy, and this was in a year when the mandated levy had just been increased. One-fifth of the districts included in the 8% had a local levy equal to the mandated (implying they would be observable at D, corresponding to a local levy of X).[14] This means that for almost all K-12 districts (as of 1966) state aid was being given as a lump-sum grant.

ESTIMATING THE EFFECTS OF STATE AID
ON EDUCATIONAL EXPENDITURES

As long as state aid is being distributed as a lump-sum grant, we can estimate the increase in expenditures if we know or can make some assumptions about the district's income elasticity of demand for education and if we know the district's income and expenditures on education.[15] Because of a lack of available income data, our estimate is limited to a total of 52 districts.[16]

The 52 districts account for approximately 48% of the

pupils in Michigan. Since the districts are all from metropolitan areas, they cannot be regarded as representative of the state, but they are adequate to demonstrate the expected effects of the current program.

The districts are viewed in terms of the 1962 state aid program and their 1962 expenditures on education. All of the districts had an observable local levy which was greater than the 8 mill mandated levy in effect for 1962.[17] With reference to Figure 13, this means that their total expenditures were all beyond a point such as D. In other words, state aid was distributed as a lump-sum grant for all of the 52 districts.

Procedure

The income elasticity for education has been defined as the percentage change in expenditures on education resulting from a one percent change in income. That is:

$$N_y = \frac{\Delta E/E}{\Delta Y/Y} = \frac{\Delta E}{\Delta Y} \frac{Y}{E}$$

What we want to know is the increase in expenditures on education resulting from state aid viewed as an increase in income. That is:

$$\Delta E = (N_y) \, E/Y \, (\Delta Y)$$

The income figure being used is family income per school child.[18] The change in income is state aid per pupil.[19] The expenditures figure being used is total operating expenditures per pupil.[20] If we can make some reasonable assumptions about what the income elasticity is likely to be we can estimate the change in expenditures on education resulting from state aid.

Two ΔE's have been estimated for each of the 52 districts: one assuming an income elasticity of .7; a second assuming an income elasticity of 1.3. The .7 and the 1.3 were chosen on the basis of previous studies, as well as some empirical work done in conjunction with the present study, and also to show the effect of allowing for some variation in the income elasticity.[21]

Results

The estimated changes in expenditures on education and the implied initial expenditures for each district are shown in Appendix 3. The mandated expenditures plus state aid (corresponding to point Z in Figure 13) are also shown for each district. As long as the mandated expenditures plus state aid figure is less than the estimated initial expenditures, the districts are at a point when state aid can be regarded only as a lump-sum grant.[22]

Since the amount of state aid varies among districts, citing various absolute values of the increase in expenditures resulting from state aid could be misleading. Instead, we will consider the estimated increase in education expenditures as a percentage of state aid. That is: $\Delta E / \Delta Y = N_y E/Y$ Expenditures on education average around 5.8% of income. With the exception of two extreme districts, education expenditures as a percentage of income (E/Y) vary between 3.5 and 8.8. The implications of the observed variation in E/Y on the increase in expenditures as a percentage of state aid is considered, first excluding the two extreme districts, and then including them.

Using the two income elasticities cited earlier and the observed variation in E/Y, we can set the boundaries on $\Delta E / \Delta Y$ for 50 of the 52 districts. This is shown by:

$$.7 \,(.035) \leq \Delta E / \Delta Y \leq 1.3 \,(.088)$$

In other words, applying the lower income elasticity to the low E/Y sets the low boundary on the estimated increase in expenditures as a percentage of state aid. Similarly, applying the higher income elasticity to the high E/Y sets the higher boundary.

The resulting estimated increase in expenditures as a percentage of state aid varies between a low of 2.5% to a high of 11.4%. If we assume that the relevant income elasticity is .7, $\Delta E/\Delta Y$ varies between 2.5% and 6.2%. If we assume 1.3 is the relevant income elasticity, $\Delta E/\Delta Y$ varies between 4.6 and 11.4%. In more familiar terms, this implies that a dollar of state aid increases educational expenditures by as little as 2.5 cents or as much as 11.4 cents.

E/Y for the two extreme districts is 10.4 and 12.1%, respectively. The reason for viewing the estimated $\Delta E/\Delta Y$ initially without these two districts was that they were the only ones more than two standard deviations away from the mean. It is not surprising that these districts exhibit such large deviations. The reason is twofold:

(1) The districts have the fourth and second lowest family income per school child, thus lowering the denominator.

(2) An estimated 90 and 91% of their taxable property value is industrial[23] (making them first and second in terms of SEV per pupil), which would lead us to expect higher expenditures on education,[24] thus increasing the numerator.

Including these two districts increases the upper boundary to 15.7%. In other words, using our high income elasticity for the most extreme district implies that a dollar of state aid is associated with an increase in education expenditures of 15.7 cents.

On the average (E/Y = 5.8%); however, a dollar of state aid is associated with an increase in education expenditures of

4.2 to 7.5 cents. Even if we were to assume an income elasticity as high as 2, the implications would be substantially the same. On the average, there would be an 11.6 cent increase in educational expenditures for every dollar of state aid.

A QUALIFICATION TO THE ESTIMATION

Under the current program, state aid to education is distributed primarily in the form of a lump-sum grant. As we have seen, this makes state aid, in effect, an untied grant. From the point of view of the district, state aid thus represents an increase in its income. As such, we can expect expenditures on education to increase. We can also expect a major portion of the grant to be taken as increased income. In other words, we can expect expenditures from local resources to be reduced. Having the school districts fiscally independent from other governmental units and having a portion of education expenditures directly responsive to the electorate is likely to facilitate the process. However, it should be clear that the reduction in expenditures from local resources is an adjustment which occurs over time and this could qualify the general implications of giving aid as a lump-sum grant. The increase in expenditures just estimated implicitly assumes that the adjustment process has had time to occur. The assumption is probably valid for the year 1962 being considered. It represents the third year of an unchanged program and followed another three-year period during which the state program had again remained the same. If, however, the state were continually to increase the amount of state aid—and, in particular, to increase it at an increasing rate—the lags in adjustment might be sufficient for a much larger portion of the grant to be channeled into education than we would otherwise expect. In general, however, we can expect state aid given as a lump-sum grant to have only a minor impact on educational expenditures.

NOTES TO CHAPTER 5

1. The use of the term "preferred position" implies that the effects of the present program are being viewed in terms of indifference curve analysis. Since the decision-making unit is the district, we are, in some sense, implying an indifference curve for the district. Indifference curve analysis is generally used for individuals rather than groups of individuals. The use of indifference curves for groups of individuals, usually as a means of obtaining a "social preference function," involves one of the problems which led to the use of indifference curve analysis in the first place—that of making interpersonal comparisons of utility. Although we are using indifference curves with reference to the district, we are not using them to define a social preference function, at least not as the term is usually used. Instead, we are just recognizing that districts do make (in fact, are forced to make) collective decisions regarding expenditures on education. It seems reasonable to assume that the district, as a collective unit, can be viewed as having preferences and establishing trade-offs between increased expenditures on education and increased disposable income.

2. The possibility that the effects of state aid could not be examined without considering some of these "other factors" was tested and rejected. For example, the present system of financing local district expenditures does not distinguish between groups of individuals who can be expected to have different allegiances to the public schools. It was thought this might affect the desired trade-offs between increased expenditures on education and increased disposable income. On the basis of a preliminary empirical analysis, it appears that if such interactions exist they are very weak ones.

3. We assume constant unit costs. We can therefore refer either to expenditures on education or to the units of education produced by a certain level of expenditures without changing the relationship between them. Throughout this section "expenditures on education" are shown on the horizontal axis rather than the traditional "quality of education" being shown there. Doing it this way facilitates the discussion.

4. Having the tax base depend on property valuation rather than

income does not in itself alter the analysis since the tax must still be paid from income. The inclusion of industrial property (given certain assumptions about the shifting of the tax) is expected to influence local district decision-making. However, the effect occurs in terms of the district's initial opportunity line and thus its initial decision regarding expenditures on education rather than the district's expected reaction to state aid.

5. At this point our partial equilibrium approach begins to present some difficulties. Viewing state aid as an addition to the district's opportunity line either implicitly assumes a "rat hole theory of taxation"—that is, taxes are collected and buried in a rat hole—or else implies some degree of double counting. If the program represented a minor part of state expenditures, we could reasonably assume that a reduction in state aid would result in an increase in another state expenditure rather than a reduction in taxes. In other words, we could assume taxes fixed. If we also assumed that the other state expenditure would not be a substitute for private-good expenditures, this would justify the treatment of state aid as an addition to the district's opportunity line. However, the state aid program is too large to make this approach tenable. But the partial approach can still be justified as long as we are considering one district at a time, rather than districts in the aggregate or all districts over time. Our assumption is that if any one district were to opt for a reduction in state taxes rather than receive state aid—with the change spread proportionately across all districts—the change in income to that one district would not be appreciable. In this case, the assumption that taxes are given is not unreasonable.

6. Portions of section one are similar to a discussion on governmental grants in Williams (1963): Chapter 10.

7. Although the effects are completely analogous to a price change, the price of education has, in fact, not been reduced. This distinction is crucial if we are to put expenditures on education rather than quantity of education on the horizontal axis without distorting the analysis.

8. The convexity assumption implies a diminishing marginal rate of substitution (MRS). The MRS refers to the rate at which the consumer would be willing to trade off one good for the other and remain just as well off. The MRS declines because as we give up income (Y) and gain education (E) the marginal utility of Y increases and the marginal utility of E declines.

9. An income elasticity expresses the relationship between changes in income and changes in the consumption of some commodity. Whenever the term "income elasticity for education" is used, it refers to the percentage change in expenditures associated with a one percent change in income. If we use ΔE and ΔY to refer to the change in expenditures and the change in income, the percentage changes in expenditures and income are $\Delta E/E$ and $\Delta Y/Y$. The income elasticity (N_y) for education is therefore: $N_y = (\Delta E/E)/(\Delta Y/Y)$

10. The only way the district could end up at Z is if the income elasticity for all other goods was zero. This is obviously untrue.

11. In the present case, there has been a change in real income, but the effect of the income increase has been restricted to expenditures on education. It therefore does not appear meaningful to view this within the usual income-substitution framework, particularly since we are led to a very different expectation—under a matching grant, we expect an increase in the amount taken as disposable income, whereas under a relevant required minimum grant we expect a decrease in the amount taken as disposable income.

12. As we already know, the current program is not simply a lump-sum grant with a required minimum. This means that the comments included in this paragraph are not directly relevant to our estimating the effects of the current program. However, the complications which arise when a district is initially between A and Q are similar to some complications which do arise under the current program.

13. We can therefore set a boundary for districts which have an observable local levy equal to the mandated amount. This is despite our general expectation that districts which are initially between X and Z will respond to the matching portion and therefore end up with an observable local levy between 2 mills under the mandated and the mandated.

14. The remaining four-fifths of the eight percent were all levying at least eight mills. This is of interest because, until 1966, eight mills was the mandated millage. There are two likely explanations for this. First, the change in the requirements made the matching portion the relevant grant which faced these districts from their already adjusted positions and they reacted accordingly. Second, at least some of the districts may not have had time to react to the change in the program. A time series analysis would be one way of testing these hypotheses. However, this would be extremely difficult to do for Michigan school

districts because of the considerable amount of district consolidation which has occurred in the past ten years. During this period, the total number of school districts decreased from around 4,800 to 1,200. In addition, the amount of information available on a school district basis is very limited.

15. This is not the way the effect of state aid has usually been estimated. For a brief critique of two of the more frequently used techniques, see Appendix 2.

16. The data available in terms of school districts primarily include property valuation, the number of pupils, and school expenditures. Since school districts rarely overlie municipalities, the census data for municipalities may poorly reflect the characteristics of the school district. Some metropolitan areas have been divided into census tracts, with data available on that basis. U. S. Department of Commerce, Bureau of the Census (1960). The 52 school districts being used here are all located in metropolitan areas for which census tract data are available. They represent the school districts which could be reasonably well approximated by a combination of tracts and for which an estimate of industrial property relative to total property could be made. The approximation has been done in Gensemer (1966).

17. The lowest local levy was 9 mills, the highest 24.9 mills, the average 15.6 mills. Michigan, State of [3].

18. This is equal to the school district's (1959) median family income divided by the district's (1960) average number of school children per family. U. S. Department of Commerce, Bureau of the Census (1960). The income figure provided by the census includes only money income. A more comprehensive measure of income would be better. For example, we might have added an estimate of imputed rental income from owner-occupied housing to money income.

19. Michigan, State of [3].

20. *Ibid.* This corresponds to our E_2 figure. Which E is appropriate (that is, E_1 or E_2) is unclear and reflects the ambiguity involved in using an arc elasticity rather than a point elasticity. The former gives the average responsiveness over some finite distance; the latter the responsiveness at a point (i.e., it is the limit of the arc elasticity). A frequently used procedure would be to take the average of E_1 and E_2, except that we don't know E_1 (although once we know ΔE, we can also

know E_1). However, it will not make very much difference which E is used when E/Y on the average is equal to 410/7200.

21. Brazer's (1959) study of per capita operating expenditures in 40 large cities as of 1952 indicated an income elasticity for education of .73.

An analysis of per pupil operating expenditures of the 52 districts indicates an income elasticity of .73. (See Appendix 4.) Gensemer's (1966: 133) study of per pupil locally financed expenditures for 55 districts (the same 52 plus 3 additional districts) indicated an income elasticity of 1.31. This difference from essentially the same data is the result of using different definitions of income, different socioeconomic variables and different measures of educational expenditures. The difference in educational expenditures is probably the most important reason, with Gensemer's figure reflecting his use of the parallel regression technique of estimation. For a critique of this technique, see Appendix 2.

While there may be some question as to whether the income elasticity is likely to be slightly above one or below one, it is unlikely to be above 1.3 or 1.5. However, the income elasticity may well vary across broad ranges of income classes. Using different values for the income elasticity implicitly allows for this possibility.

22. This is true for all 52 districts, but it is determined, in large part, by the assumptions used in calculating the ΔE's.

23. The estimates are based on data for the municipalities which overlie the districts. Data sources are Michigan Municipal League *Financial Abstracts* (1963): Volume II; and Detroit Metropolitan Area Regional Planning Commission (1959): 119, in Gensemer (1966).

24. Under the present system, local districts have the right (and the constitutional obligation) to impose the same tax rates on industrial property as they do on residential property. The implications of this depend on the degree to which the tax is shifted or at least the residents' perception of the incidence of the tax. In principle, the tax could be shifted backward to the suppliers of labor and capital or forward to the consumers. If, for example, we can assume that labor and capital are moderately mobile and that the industry is selling in a national market, most of the tax remains on the site value of the land. (Brazer, 1961b: 139.)

As long as the residents, as suppliers of labor or as consumers, do not pay the tax (or perceive of themselves as paying it), the presence of industrial property lowers the "price" of education in a manner analogous to the matching grant. We would therefore expect that the presence of industrial property would be associated with higher expenditures on education. An analysis of the per pupil operating expenditures (Appendix 4) indicates that on the average a one point increase in the percentage of property classified as industrial is associated with an increase in expenditures of $3.10. Districts with 90 and 91% of their property industrial can therefore be expected to have very high expenditures on education.

Chapter **6**

CONCLUSIONS & POLICY IMPLICATIONS

The purpose of Chapter 6 is to consider the policy implications of the theoretical analysis in Chapter 5, given the general framework, and state objectives established earlier. First, however, our evaluation of both the Michigan program and the general concept of a foundation program needs to be completed.

As before, the Michigan program is being evaluated primarily in terms of its own objectives. This time, however, our concern is with the means used to accomplish these objectives.

A major objective of the program is to equalize educational opportunity, which has been interpreted to mean equalizing the availability of educational services. A secondary objective is to increase the level of educational services in general. Again, assuming a direct relationship between expenditures on education and quality of educational services provided, the purpose of the state grant is to increase the district's expenditures on education.

State aid in Michigan is distributed by means of a foundation program. The standard foundation program involves a required contribution from the district and a lump-sum grant from the state.

The effect of the program depends on whether the required local contribution is less than or greater than the amount that would otherwise be spent. If it is less, as it appears to be for almost all districts in Michigan, the lump-sum part of the program is the only relevant one. If it is greater, the required local contribution part of the program is the relevant part, and it plays a "stimulative minimum" role. As a lump-sum grant, it represents the least efficient way of increasing expenditures on education.[1] The reason is that a lump-sum grant only affects the resources available to the district;[2] it does not alter the attractiveness of expenditures on education as opposed to expenditures on anything else. In other words, relative prices remain the same. A stimulative minimum grant, on the other hand, represents a very efficient way of increasing expenditures on education, because a required local minimum produces a kink in the price line. The kink, in turn, accentuates the change in relative prices which occurs at that point, thus increasing the incentive for the district to raise its expenditures from local resources to the required local minimum.

There are disadvantages to both types of grants. The lump-sum grant is inefficient. The stimulative minimum grant is efficient, but attempting to induce an increase in expenditures from local resources introduces the possibility that the district may choose not to participate. If increasing district expenditures on education is the major objective, this is obviously a serious drawback. Even if most districts do participate, the amount by which the local resources available for other goods is reduced is likely to vary among communities. The use of a stimulative minimum grant may therefore accentuate any existing inequalities in the distribution of resources among communities. Furthermore, under a foundation program, it is likely that the grant either will be a lump-sum grant for all districts or a stimulative minimum grant for some districts and a lump-sum grant for the remaining districts. This occurs because a single millage rate is used to determine the required local contribution. It is difficult to regard a program consisting of a stimulative minimum grant for some districts and a lump-sum grant for others as being much of an improvement over a lump-sum grant for all. While it would improve the efficiency of the program for the first group of districts, provided they participate, it would result in a differential "excess burden" between the two groups.[3]

The major defect of the foundation program is, therefore, that its structure is inappropriate to the fulfillment of its own objectives. Thus, the fundamental criticism of the current Michigan program is not that it is deficient as a foundation program but that it *is* a foundation program.

GENERAL OBJECTIVES

The major objective of the Michigan program, equalizing educational opportunity, can be viewed within the general framework developed in Chapter 1.

In establishing a general framework, two aspects of intergovernmental grants were considered: allocative efficiency and interpersonal income redistribution.

The general conclusions were that intergovernmental grants can be used to compensate for externalities in the allocation of resources to education and that grants to education both affect the distribution of future income and can be deliberately used for that purpose.

The objective of equalizing educational opportunity can be viewed as one form of a redistributive policy although it might be more appropriately considered under the general heading of "equity."[4] The equalization of educational opportunity can be expected to affect the future distribution of income, but these effects will not necessarily coincide with the desired effects of a specific redistributive policy. The use of education as a means of redistributing future income presumably depends on educational achievement rather than on educational opportunity. Since educational achievement appears to be strongly related to a student's socioeconomic background,[5] attaining the level of achievement needed for the fulfillment of a redistributive objective may require the provision of unequal educational opportunities.

Although there may be some conflict between the equalization of educational opportunity and the fulfillment of a particular redistributive objective, the conflict is unlikely to be a serious one. The intention of the equalization objective is the provision of more equal rather than absolutely equal educational opportunities. In addition, the term "opportunity" is frequently defined so as to include "achievement" or even so as to be synonymous with it.[6] Using the term "educational opportunity" to include "educational achievement" ignores the distinction between the inputs (the student and all the other inputs which are a part of the educational process) and the output (educational achievement) of the educational process. However, if achievement is included within the measure of opportunity, and if students differ in their ability, motivation, and out-of-school education (which they do), then any attempt to equalize educational opportunity either will be unsuccessful or will imply unequal educational opportunity as the term has been used here. With this definition of opportunity, however, it is unlikely that there would be any conflict between the equalization objective and a redistributive objective.

Since opportunity is frequently used to include achievement, it appears that "equalizing achievement" is also of concern. Rather than include or imply achievement within the concept of opportunity, we shall consider "equalizing achievement" (defined in terms of avoiding unacceptable differences in achievement) as an additional objective.[7]

IMPLICATIONS OF THE OBJECTIVES

Thus, there are still basically two issues which are of concern in developing a program of aid to education: alloca-

nd, other things being equal, the greater the ex
ease in expenditures on education.[15] In terms o
s presented in Chapter 5, increasing the matchin
a pivoting of the district's price line to the right
er, if the pivoting occurs from the intercept
es that the matching begins with the first dollar o
ditures, it is likely to become very costly to
thing more than a minor increase in educationa
s. As was noted earlier, we can expect that with a
rant total expenditures, given reasonable assump-
income and price elasticities, will increase, but by
which is less than the amount of state aid. (In
igure 9, we expect the district to move in a
y direction.) In other words, the grant will be
local resources for expenditures on "other goods"
creasing expenditures on education.

gh a matching grant is more efficient than a lump
it still may not be very efficient. The inefficiency,
re the factor which would make this type of
stly, results from the district's freedom to substi-
itures on other goods for expenditures on educa-
we want, therefore, is a system of grants which
e the degree of substitutability between education
oods. Conceptually, this could be accomplished by
he matching grant to expenditures which are great-
district's initial expenditures. In other words, the
ould be pivoted from a district's E_1 position (or
nation of that position), rather than from the
ping this will not eliminate the district's freedom
stitutions, so we would still expect that some of
ould be used to free local resources for other
t by not matching for an initial level of expendi-
te is able to offer a far larger matching rate than
erwise. This implies a larger increase in expendi-
could be expected if the state were to use a

tive efficiency; and distributional or equity objectives. The distributional or equity objectives are reflected in the "equalizing educational opportunity" and "equalizing educational achievement" objectives. Equalizing educational opportunity implies that educational expenditures should be increased in those districts which provide less education than other districts. Equalizing educational achievement implies that educational expenditures should be relatively higher in those districts which will require a greater amount of educational inputs in order to produce a given amount of achievement.[8] As noted, there is some conflict between these objectives. To the extent that increased education is being used as a means of redistributing future income or that equalization of achievement reflects a policy of equity, the unequal opportunity implication of this objective would supersede the objective of equal educational opportunity.

The allocative efficiency objective is reflected in our concern with the benefit spillovers associated with education. Allocative efficiency requires that expenditures on education should be increased wherever marginal social benefits are greater than marginal private benefits. However, our concern is with spillovers between governmental units. Within this context, allocative efficiency requires that expenditures on education should be increased in any district where marginal external benefits are greater than marginal internal benefits.[9] In the first chapter, some evidence was cited suggesting that the benefit spillovers were greater where educational expenditures were less (which in turn implied a grant inversely related to "wealth"). In part, this reflected the potential reduction in welfare costs, which can only be considered a spillover on the assumption of a given distributional policy. This obviously overlaps the use of education as a means of redistributing future income.[10]

An additional reason for increasing educational expenditures where less education is provided was based on the general expectation that the rate of return (including both internal and external benefits) is greater, at the margin, where expenditures are less. It is possible, however, that social benefits (exclusive of benefits reflecting redistributive or equity objectives) are greater in high socioeconomic communities which already spend relatively more on education, implying that expenditures should be increased in these communities. Excluding redistributive or equity objectives, it is unclear how the spillovers vary with variations in the level of education already being provided. For present purposes, it is assumed that some spillovers exist at all levels of expenditures, thus implying that expenditures on education should be increased to some extent in all districts.

POLICY IMPLICATIONS

The concluding section of this study is concerned with the policy implications of the preceding analyses. The policy implications are considered first on a general level and then incorporated in an illustrative program.

If we knew the optimum level[11] of educational expenditures (E^*) for each district, and if we knew and could continue to know what the district's position would be in the absence of state aid (E_1), an efficient way of obtaining the optimal expenditures would be through the use of conditional lump-sum grants. For example, the program could be designed so that each district would receive $E^* - E_1$, subject to the condition that the district spends E_1 of its own resources on education. However, as long as the additional education results in some positive utility to the district, the program could be made more efficient by offering the district less than $E^* - E_1$ and requiring it to spend more than E_1 of its own resources. The least-cost way for the state to achieve E^* would be to set the required local expenditures at the level which would move the district out along its indifference curve from E_1.

Our knowledge about
initial positions, and the c
obviously less than perfect
general objectives of aid to
these objectives establish t
This is to increase expendi
tricts and to a greater exte
less than is provided elsewh
of educational inputs to ob
What remains to be develop
both efficient and effective.

Alternative Instruments

Three types of grants
lump-sum grant, the stimu
matching grant. In comple
program, both the lump-su
mum grant were found
lump-sum grant is effective
tive minimum grant is very
possibility of nonparticipat

The matching grant re
other two grants in term
effectiveness of a lump-su
efficient than a stimulative
tive because it eliminates
The matching grant is m
because, in addition to in
mand over resources availa
price of education.

The increase in a dis
matching grant depends t
the program and the dist
education (analogous to t
er).[14] The larger the rate

reduction
pected in
the diagra
rate impli
How
which im
local exp
achieve ar
expenditu
matching
tions abou
an amoun
terms of
northeaste
used to fre
as well as
Altho
-sum grant
and there
program c
tute expen
tion. What
will minim
and other
restricting
er than the
price line
an approxi
intercept. I
to make su
the grant
purposes. B
tures, the s
it could ot
tures than

straight matching program.[16] There would be an even greater incentive for the district to increase its expenditures on education if the state were to increase the rate of matching as the district increased its expenditures beyond its initial position.[17] This in turn would reduce the degree of substitution even further.

Thus a system of matching grants under which the matching begins at or near the initial position provides an efficient and effective policy instrument at a conceptual level. The obvious difficulty in making the system operational is in ascertaining the initial position. Attempting to make too close an approximation of E_1 introduces the possibility of overstating it. In this case, the grant becomes a stimulative-minimum grant and the advantage of making some compromise in efficiency in order to obtain effectiveness has been lost. Thus, to retain effectiveness the level at which to begin matching must be understated rather than overstated. This is especially true for the districts the state is most concerned to have participate. As long as the beginning level is greater than zero, the grant is more efficient than a straight matching grant. The closer the beginning level is to the initial position, the more efficient the grant. The closer the beginning level is to zero, the greater the district's ability to substitute between education and other goods, and therefore the less efficient the grant. Making use of the available data regarding the important correlates of educational expenditures will make it easier to establish appropriate beginning levels.

An Illustrative Program

The program outlined below is based on the policy implications of the theoretical analysis and on the general objectives discussed earlier, but it is primarily intended to be illustrative.

There are two decisions to be made in establishing the type of program just described:

(1) The level of local expenditures at which to begin the matching; and

(2) The rate at which to match.

Beginning level: The main concern in choosing the beginning level is that it be greater than zero and less than an estimate of the district's initial expenditures. As a safety measure, it seems advisable to understate the beginning level even though doing so will decrease the efficiency of the grant.

Resource availability, defined both in terms of family income and the percentage of property classified as industrial, appears to be a major correlate of expenditures on education.[18] Since taxable capacity tends to be high, either because the district's level of family income is high or because a substantial percentage of property is industrial, taxable capacity can be used as a proxy for the level at which to begin the matching.[19] Establishing the beginning level in terms of a constant millage provides a substantial amount of variation in the dollar value of that level. Small increases in the millage rate, as taxable capacity increases, provide even greater variance. This approach is used in the illustrative program.

Matching rate: The second and more important decision, in terms of increasing the district's expenditures on education, involves the rate at which to match. Since it is assumed that benefits external to residents of the district exist at all levels of expenditures, some matching should be provided for all districts. The equal educational opportunity objective implies that expenditures should be increased in districts which provide less than is considered acceptable. This implies a matching rate which is inversely related to taxable capacity. The equalizing achievement objective implies that expenditures should be increased by a relatively larger amount in districts

reduction and, other things being equal, the greater the e.
pected increase in expenditures on education.[15] In terms o
the diagrams presented in Chapter 5, increasing the matching
rate implies a pivoting of the district's price line to the right.

However, if the pivoting occurs from the intercept,
which implies that the matching begins with the first dollar of
local expenditures, it is likely to become very costly to
achieve anything more than a minor increase in educational
expenditures. As was noted earlier, we can expect that with a
matching grant total expenditures, given reasonable assumptions about income and price elasticities, will increase, but by
an amount which is less than the amount of state aid. (In
terms of Figure 9, we expect the district to move in a
northeasterly direction.) In other words, the grant will be
used to free local resources for expenditures on "other goods"
as well as increasing expenditures on education.

Although a matching grant is more efficient than a lump
-sum grant, it still may not be very efficient. The inefficiency,
and therefore the factor which would make this type of
program costly, results from the district's freedom to substitute expenditures on other goods for expenditures on education. What we want, therefore, is a system of grants which
will minimize the degree of substitutability between education
and other goods. Conceptually, this could be accomplished by
restricting the matching grant to expenditures which are greater than the district's initial expenditures. In other words, the
price line would be pivoted from a district's E_1 position (or
an approximation of that position), rather than from the
intercept. Doing this will not eliminate the district's freedom
to make substitutions, so we would still expect that some of
the grant would be used to free local resources for other
purposes. But by not matching for an initial level of expenditures, the state is able to offer a far larger matching rate than
it could otherwise. This implies a larger increase in expenditures than could be expected if the state were to use a

Our knowledge about optimum levels of expenditures, initial positions, and the corresponding indifference curves is obviously less than perfect. However, the discussion of the general objectives of aid to education and the implications of these objectives establish the basic purpose of the program. This is to increase expenditures, to some extent, in all districts and to a greater extent in those districts which provide less than is provided elsewhere or which require a greater level of educational inputs to obtain a given level of achievement. What remains to be developed is a policy instrument which is both efficient and effective.[1 2]

Alternative Instruments

Three types of grants were considered in Chapter 5: the lump-sum grant, the stimulative minimum grant,[1 3] and the matching grant. In completing the evaluation of a foundation program, both the lump-sum grant and the stimulative minimum grant were found to have serious deficiencies. The lump-sum grant is effective but very inefficient. The stimulative minimum grant is very efficient but, because it raises the possibility of nonparticipation, may be ineffective.

The matching grant represents a compromise between the other two grants in terms of efficiency while retaining the effectiveness of a lump-sum grant. The matching grant is less efficient than a stimulative minimum grant but is more effective because it eliminates the possibility of nonparticipation. The matching grant is more efficient than a lump-sum grant because, in addition to increasing income (by increasing command over resources available for all purposes), it reduces the price of education.

The increase in a district's expenditures resulting from a matching grant depends both on the matching provisions of the program and the district's price elasticity of demand for education (analogous to the income elasticity discussed earlier).[1 4] The larger the rate of matching, the greater the "price"

tive efficiency; and distributional or equity objectives. The distributional or equity objectives are reflected in the "equalizing educational opportunity" and "equalizing educational achievement" objectives. Equalizing educational opportunity implies that educational expenditures should be increased in those districts which provide less education than other districts. Equalizing educational achievement implies that educational expenditures should be relatively higher in those districts which will require a greater amount of educational inputs in order to produce a given amount of achievement.[8] As noted, there is some conflict between these objectives. To the extent that increased education is being used as a means of redistributing future income or that equalization of achievement reflects a policy of equity, the unequal opportunity implication of this objective would supersede the objective of equal educational opportunity.

The allocative efficiency objective is reflected in our concern with the benefit spillovers associated with education. Allocative efficiency requires that expenditures on education should be increased wherever marginal social benefits are greater than marginal private benefits. However, our concern is with spillovers between governmental units. Within this context, allocative efficiency requires that expenditures on education should be increased in any district where marginal external benefits are greater than marginal internal benefits.[9] In the first chapter, some evidence was cited suggesting that the benefit spillovers were greater where educational expenditures were less (which in turn implied a grant inversely related to "wealth"). In part, this reflected the potential reduction in welfare costs, which can only be considered a spillover on the assumption of a given distributional policy. This obviously overlaps the use of education as a means of redistributing future income.[10]

An additional reason for increasing educational expenditures where less education is provided was based on the general expectation that the rate of return (including both internal and external benefits) is greater, at the margin, where expenditures are less. It is possible, however, that social benefits (exclusive of benefits reflecting redistributive or equity objectives) are greater in high socioeconomic communities which already spend relatively more on education, implying that expenditures should be increased in these communities. Excluding redistributive or equity objectives, it is unclear how the spillovers vary with variations in the level of education already being provided. For present purposes, it is assumed that some spillovers exist at all levels of expenditures, thus implying that expenditures on education should be increased to some extent in all districts.

POLICY IMPLICATIONS

The concluding section of this study is concerned with the policy implications of the preceding analyses. The policy implications are considered first on a general level and then incorporated in an illustrative program.

If we knew the optimum level[11] of educational expenditures (E^*) for each district, and if we knew and could continue to know what the district's position would be in the absence of state aid (E_1), an efficient way of obtaining the optimal expenditures would be through the use of conditional lump-sum grants. For example, the program could be designed so that each district would receive $E^* - E_1$, subject to the condition that the district spends E_1 of its own resources on education. However, as long as the additional education results in some positive utility to the district, the program could be made more efficient by offering the district less than $E^* - E_1$ and requiring it to spend more than E_1 of its own resources. The least—cost way for the state to achieve E^* would be to set the required local expenditures at the level which would move the district out along its indifference curve from E_1.

which require a higher quality of educational inputs in order to produce a given level of achievement. The general assumption is that this applies to children from a low socioeconomic level. In some districts, this may be associated with low taxable capacity but in many others it probably is not.

An unlimited number of matching programs could be devised, each having different variations in the rate of matching across districts and perhaps also different variations in the rate of matching across expenditures in any one district.[20] The table below provides one example.

TABLE 6

ILLUSTRATIVE MATCHING PROGRAM

District Per Pupil SEV	Beginning Level		Matching Rate
($)	(Mills)	($)	
5,000	10	50	9.00
10,000	10	100	2.25
20,000	10	200	.56
30,000	11	330	.25
40,000	12	480	.14
50,000	13	650	.09

In the illustrative program, the beginning level remains at 10 mills up to a per pupil SEV of $20,000. For districts with a per pupil SEV of $20,000 to $50,000, the initiating level increases continuously from 10 mills to 13 mills. The formula for the matching rate is equal to: $(\$15,000/SEV)^2$, except that the matching rate is fixed at 9 for all districts with a per pupil SEV of less than $5,000. The matching rate increases rapidly as the per pupil SEV falls to low levels and decreases slowly as the per pupil SEV rises to high levels.

Estimating the effects of the program on a district's expenditures on education and on the amount of state aid it receives (and thus the cost of the program) requires specific information on a district by district basis. No attempt is made here to estimate the overall effects of the illustrative program. However, the effects for any given district can be estimated without great difficulty and the process of estimation will indicate how an estimate of the effects for all districts could be made. More importantly, it will allow us to compare the effects of the type of program being illustrated with the expected effects of the current program.

To estimate the effects of the illustrative program, the following are needed or are to be found:

ΔE = increase in expenditures on education resulting from state aid (This includes the local expenditures matched [LEM] plus the state aid associated with them.)

TE = total expenditures

SA = state aid

$\Delta E = N_P \, (\Delta P/P) \, (E_1 - E_{BL})$

where P = price, N_P = price elasticity, ΔP = change in price, E_1 = initial expenditures, and E_{BL} = expenditures associated with the beginning level of the matching grant.

The estimation is for a district with a per pupil SEV of $12,000. ΔP is equal to -.61. P is equal to .7.[21] N_P is assumed equal to .5 (from Appendix 4). E_1 is assumed equal to 379.4 (from Appendix 3). E_{BL} is equal to 120. Therefore:

$\Delta E = 112.8$

$TE = E_1 + \Delta E$

$\quad = 492.2$

$SA = [MR/(1 + MR)] (TE\text{-}BL)^{22}$

where MR = matching rate. The matching rate is 1.56. Therefore: SA = 227.0

Thus, an increase in expenditures on education of 112.8 is associated with state aid equal to 227.0. As discussed earlier, when the matching begins below the initial position, we can expect that there will be an increase in expenditures on education but that expenditures on "other goods" will also increase.

The more important point, however, is to compare the estimated increase associated with the same amount of state aid distributed under the current program. In this case, $\Delta E = (N_y) E/Y(\Delta Y)$. E/Y for this district is equal to .056. $\Delta Y = 227.0$. If we use an income elasticity of 1.3: $\Delta E = 16.5$ Thus, for the same amount of state aid, the estimated increase in expenditures on education is \$112.80 under the illustrative program and \$16.50 when state aid is distributed as a lump-sum grant, as it appears to be for almost all districts under the current program.

It is not possible to look at the experience of other states as a means of estimating the effects of the type of program just described. The closest approximation currently in use is the percentage equalizing grant. The basic features of the grant are similar to the program suggested here: the state pays some share of the district's locally determined expenditures and the state's share is larger in poor districts than it is in rich districts. As of 1964, however, Wisconsin and Rhode Island were the only states using a percentage equalizing grant and only Wisconsin had been using it for more than a few years. As a possible reflection of the program's effectiveness, educational expenditures relative to state personal income and educational expenditures per pupil relative to per capita income have increased more in Wisconsin than they have nationally.[23]

CONCLUDING COMMENTS

In developing the illustrative program it has been assumed that equity or redistributive objectives are dominant factors in determining the distribution of aid to education. It is possible that the maximization of objectively valued net benefits would imply that expenditures should be increased in high socioeconomic communities. In this case, the choice among objectives would depend, in large part, on value judgments rather than on narrowly defined efficiency considerations. Once such decisions have been made, however, efficiency in accomplishing the objective is highly desirable. The cost of inefficiency is to jeopardize the accomplishment of whatever objective has been set or reduce the extent to which it may be achieved under a given budget constraint.

Although the type of program suggested is an effective mechanism for increasing a district's expenditures on education, increased expenditures will not necessarily further the equalization of achievement. Nor is it known what would be necessary. A major problem may be that a system of grants made on a district basis is not appropriate to the fulfillment of this objective. The difficulties in operating at the district level are likely to be particularly acute in the central cities. Within these areas, neighborhoods and therefore neighborhood schools are generally highly homogeneous in terms of socio economic characteristics of their pupils. As a result, the need for differential amounts of education may be as great within a school district as between districts. Nor is it likely that a significant equalization of achievement can occur without a major change in the "disadvantaged" child's total environment.

Thus some of the most pressing problems may remain outside the sphere of a program of state aid to education, including the one developed here. However, the adoption of a state aid program suitable to its own objectives could permit the achievement of the equalization of educational opportunity objective. To a lesser extent, it may facilitate the equalization of educational achievement as well.

NOTES TO CHAPTER 6

1. Efficient in the sense of maximizing the increase in expenditures from a given amount of aid.

2. Altering resource availability may be an objective, but it cannot be accomplished effectively by means of a grant to education. A major reason is that the grant is much too small. See page 28 above.

3. The "excess burden" refers to the distortion in resource allocation relative to local preferences associated with a tax or expenditure policy which changes relative prices. The distortion in this case results from the kink in the price line. There is no excess burden associated with the lump-sum grant. The absence of excess burden allows a district to reach a more preferred position relative to its own preferences under a lump-sum grant than it can under a grant which changes the price of education relative to other goods.

4. The term "equity" is used here to cover a variety of objectives reflecting a society's concept of justice or fairness in its treatment of individuals. The desired distribution of income would therefore be included within the concept of equity. A policy is considered a redistribu-

tive policy if its primary intent is to alter the distribution of income. Since a single policy may be used specifically as a means of redistributing income and also be a reflection of society's concept of justice, the choice of terms at times becomes arbitrary.

5. For example, see Burkhead et al. (1967): 88; Burkhead and Campbell (1968): 612; Coleman Report (1966): 21.

6. See, for example, Coleman Report (1966): 20.

7. The objective of equalizing educational achievement is assumed to be a proxy for existing redistributive policies as well as representing a policy of equity.

8. It is implicitly assumed that an increase in expenditures can have a positive influence on educational achievement. This assumption is contrary to the findings of the Coleman Report, which found that there is very little relation between per pupil expenditures or educational facilities and achievement, once socioeconomic background is controlled. The important factors are the student's own socioeconomic background and that of his peers. Coleman Report (1966): 325.

There are two reasons for continuing the assumption of a positive relationship between expenditures and achievement:

First, both the measurement of the variables and the statistical techniques used in the Coleman Report have been subject to serious criticism. Some of the major criticisms include: the use of a per pupil instructional expenditure figure which is based on the average for the school district; the limited range of educational facilities measured; and the measurement of the unique contribution of each variable in terms of the addition to the proportion of variance explained by each variable, in a situation where the crucial variables are highly intercorrelated. In this case, the importance of the variable used first is overstated; that which is second, understated. Since background was the variable used first, it is not very surprising that socioeconomic background explains more of the variance. For further discussion, see Bowles and Levin (1968): 3-24.

Second, our assumption requires only that an increase in the quantity and/or quality of inputs entering the educational process could compensate for at least some deficiencies in the student input and that this increase in inputs would be reflected in higher expenditures. It does not require that any given increase in expenditures is necessarily associated with higher achievement.

9. Internal benefits include both private benefits and intracommunity spillovers. External benefits refer to intercommunity spillovers.

The internal-external benefit distinction is used here in contrast to the usual distinction between social benefits (all spillovers) and private benefits.

10. In fact, as long as we define benefits in terms of subjective evaluation (the utility or satisfaction which accrues to an individual from the consumption of a good) rather than an objective evaluation (the dollar value of benefits associated with any good), the redistributive or equity goals are already included in determining the output where marginal social benefits equal marginal social costs. In other words, we can view a desire to provide, say, equal educational opportunity as implying that individuals (other than those directly benefiting) would derive satisfaction or utility from the provision of equal educational opportunity.

11. Optimum in terms of equity or distributional objectives and allocative efficiency.

12. An effective policy is one which accomplishes the objective of the program which, in this case, is increasing expenditures on education.

13. In Chapter 5, this was discussed in terms of a matching grant subject to a required local contribution. The distinguishing feature of the grant, however, is that the required contribution is greater than the amount that would otherwise be spent. The district either will not participate or will move to the point corresponding to the required minimum. The type of grant which accompanies the stimulative minimum is irrelevant.

14. Estimating the expected increase in expenditure from a matching grant would be similar to the estimation of the increase resulting from a lump-sum grant described in Chapter 5. In this case, $\Delta E = N_p(\Delta P/P)E$ where N_p equals the price elasticity and ΔP equals the change in price.

15. This is true if "all other things" remain equal. However, the district's price elasticity of demand for education may vary with variations in price. In this case, the increase in expenditures associated with an increase in the matching rate could be offset by the decrease in expenditures associated with a lower price elasticity.

16. Although the state could increase expenditures to the same level with the use of a straight matching program, the existence of budget constraints would make this extremely unlikely.

17. This would appear diagrammatically as a series of rightward kinks in the price line.

18. See Notes to Chapter 1, footnote 20, and Appendix 4.

19. Because of the possibility that the residents, as suppliers of labor capital and land or consumers, may not bear the tax on industrial property, the presence of industrial property may have different implications regarding the "burden" of supporting education relative to an area with the same taxable capacity but with little or no industrial property. Income and the percentage of property industrial, however, are of similar importance as explanatory variables, as evidenced by their similar coefficients of partial correlation. (See Appendix 4.) It is the second point which is of concern in establishing the beginning level.

20. An example of a program in which the matching rate would vary across districts and across expenditures in any one district is given by the following:

All districts begin matching at 10 mills.

The initial matching rates range from 4 for a district with a per pupil SEV of $5,000 to .25 for a district with a per pupil SEV of $30,000.

The matching rate for the $5,000 SEV district is 4 for the first $20 above 10 mills, 4.15 for the next $25, 4.30 for the next $25, and so forth.

The matching rate for the $30,000 district is .25 for the first $20 above 10 mills, .35 for the next $25, .45 for the next $25, and so forth.

21. As mentioned previously, when an arc elasticity is used, it is unclear whether P is equal to P_0 or P_1. In this case, the choice is between P equal to .39 or 1.0. The frequent procedure of taking the average has been followed. Thus, $(P_0 + P_1)/2 = .7$.

22. We begin with the identity total expenditures minus the beginning level of expenditures equals state aid plus local expenditures matched

$$TE - BL = SA + LEM$$

State aid under a matching program equals local expenditures matched times the matching rate

$$TE - BL = MR (LEM) + LEM$$

Further manipulation of the terms yields the following:

$$TE - BL = (LEM) (1 + MR)$$
$$MR [(TE - BL)/(1 + MR)] = (LEM) (MR)$$
$$[MR/(1 + MR)] (TE - BL) = SA$$

23. Burkhead (1964): 214-228.

APPENDICES

APPENDIX 1
ACCUMULATED PAYMENTS UNDER ALTERNATIVE STATE AID PROGRAMS[a]

Accumulated Pupils (in percentage)	Accumulated Payments (in percentage)			
	Program 1	Program 2	Program 3	Program 4
2.62	3.177	3.674	3.646	4.275
5.33	6.373	7.262	7.248	8.417
8.09	9.595	10.837	10.853	12.533
10.46	12.903	14.467	14.530	16.701
13.60	15.926	17.755	17.872	20.466
16.38	19.083	21.151	21.339	24.344
19.03	22.071	24.342	24.607	27.980
21.68	25.023	27.461	27.814	31.521
24.87	28.567	31.180	31.650	35.742
27.57	31.542	34.271	34.850	39.236
30.32	34.547	37.365	38.066	42.710
32.94	37.384	40.252	41.080	45.969
35.58	40.209	43.082	44.055	49.135
38.23	43.023	45.873	47.001	52.249
41.08	46.021	48.809	50.118	55.512
44.52	49.597	52.266	53.807	59.337
47.23	52.405	54.951	56.686	62.299
49.92	55.158	57.562	59.490	65.159
52.57	57.838	60.098	62.189	67.869
56.69	61.891	63.934	66.172	71.735
59.36	64.446	66.352	68.626	74.037
62.33	67.250	69.006	71.277	76.463
65.58	70.273	71.867	74.100	78.994
70.57	74.860	76.208	78.338	82.716
87.23	89.999	90.536	92.150	94.624
90.00	92.480	92.883	94.375	97.663
92.77	94.913	95.186	96.512	98.200
95.59	97.255	97.402	98.445	99.560
98.91	99.564	99.588	99.890	100.000
100.00	100.000	100.000	100.000	100.000

a. The accumulation was done in terms of the number of pupils and the dollars of state aid, accumulating from low to high for each. The accumulated pupils and the corresponding accumulated payments were recorded at intervals of 50,000 pupils or as close to 50,000 as was possible without splitting districts. After the numbers were accumulated, the corresponding percentages were calculated.

APPENDIX 2
CRITIQUE OF
PARALLEL REGRESSION AND MULTIPLE REGRESSION
TECHNIQUES OF ESTIMATION

Two statistical methods of estimating the influence of state aid on expenditures for public education have been used in previous studies. This appendix discusses the inherent weakness of each of these approaches and thus explains why a statistical estimate of the influence of state aid on expenditures for public education has not been included in this study.

One statistical technique involves use of a pair of parallel regressions.[1] The technique is to regress two dependent variables which differ from each other by the amount of state aid on the same independent variables. The coefficients of the independent variables are then examined and the elasticity of the dependent variable with respect to the independent variable calculated. As an example, we can assume the following: one of the independent variables is median family income, the elasticity of local expenditures per pupil with respect to median family income is 2.0, and the elasticity of total operating expenditures per pupil with respect to median family income is .7. The conclusion would be that the effect of state aid is to decrease greatly the influence of median family income on per pupil expenditures. Therefore, state aid is equalizing.

The technique of parallel regression depends on one crucial assumption. It assumes that local expenditures in the absence of state aid would be the same as local expenditures with state aid. In Chapter 5 it was argued that state aid to

Michigan school districts is primarily distributed as a lump-sum grant. The increase in expenditures associated with this type of grant depends on the income elasticity of demand for education. Even assuming fairly high values for the income elasticity, it was demonstrated that only a small proportion of the grant is used to increase expenditures on education. The larger proportion is used to decrease local expenditures for education. Local expenditures in the absence of state aid are therefore expected to be much closer to total expenditures than to total expenditures less state aid. The crucial assumption behind the parallel regression method is therefore especially invalid for Michigan. Furthermore, the assumption that local expenditures in the absence of state aid would be the same as local expenditures with state aid, except by chance, is contrary to expectations from economic theory, irrespective of the type of grant being used. This technique does not therefore represent a useful way of estimating the influence of state aid on educational expenditures.

A second approach to estimating the influence of state aid is to include state aid as a dependent variable in a multiple regression analysis.[2] As already noted, the largest share of state aid is determined by taxable capacity. State aid is therefore highly correlated with taxable capacity. Taxable capacity (or a proxy for it), however, appears to be an important correlate of educational expenditures.[3]

If taxable capacity is omitted and only state aid is included as an explanatory variable, the resulting negative coefficient cannot be interpreted. It is meaningless to argue that an increase of one dollar in state aid would lead to a decrease in total expenditures. What has happened is that state aid has become a proxy for taxable capacity. An increase in state aid implies there is a decrease in taxable capacity and, as we would expect, a district with less taxable capacity spends less. If both state aid and taxable capacity are included, the results are again useless. This was done as part of a preliminary analysis of the 52 Michigan school districts considered in Chapter 5. The resulting state aid coefficient was still negative (and therefore meaningless). However, even if it were not, the high degree of intercorrelation would make any interpretation of the coefficients questionable.

The conclusion is that state aid, being highly correlated with factors which influence educational expenditures, cannot be meaningfully included as an independent variable in a multiple regression analysis.

NOTES TO APPENDIX 2

1. Miner (1963).

2. See, for example, Bishop (1964); Renshaw (1960): 170-174; Sacks and Harris (1964): 75-85.

3. Resource availability, rather than taxable capacity, logically would be the important explanatory variable with respect to educational expenditures. However, taxable capacity tends to be higher when resource availability, defined in terms of family income and the presence of industrial property, is high. The term taxable capacity can therefore be regarded as a proxy for resource availability.

APPENDIX 3

ESTIMATED EFFECTS OF THE 1962 PROGRAM

School District	(1) Total Operating Expenditures (per pupil) ($)	(2) Expenditures Income	(3) ΔE^a if $Ny^b = .7$ ($)	(4) ΔE if $Ny = 1.3$ ($)	(5) E_1^c if $Ny = .7$ $(1) - (3)$ ($)	(6) E_1 if $Ny = 1.3$ $(1) - (4)$ ($)	(7) Mandated Expenditures Plus State Aid ($)
#01 Bay City	294.6	.048	5.3	9.9	289.3	284.7	272.6
06 Flint City	326.7	.047	4.7	8.7	322.0	318.0	295.7
12 East Lansing	384.2	.039	4.2	7.8	380.0	367.4	282.7
13 Lansing City	406.6	.058	5.9	11.0	400.7	395.6	290.6
14 Jackson City Union	410.7	.056	5.9	11.0	404.8	399.7	284.5
15 Kalamazoo #1	525.0	.073	7.3	13.6	517.7	511.4	295.6
17 E. Grand Rapids	423.0	.041	4.4	8.2	418.6	414.8	280.7
18 Godwin Heights	379.2	.062	6.5	12.1	372.7	367.1	287.8
19 Grand Rapids City	369.5	.055	5.4	10.0	364.1	359.5	302.7
21 Centerline City	372.3	.045	4.8	8.9	367.5	363.4	282.9
22 East Detroit	361.5	.051	6.1	11.4	355.4	350.1	254.1
23 Fitzgerald	493.7	.067	5.2	9.7	488.5	484.0	341.9
26 Lake Shore	320.2	.042	5.0	9.3	315.2	310.9	242.5
27 Lakeview	367.3	.049	5.9	10.9	361.4	356.4	254.0
28 Mt. Clemens Comm.	318.5	.052	6.3	11.6	312.2	306.9	253.5
29 Roseville City	310.2	.055	7.1	13.1	303.1	297.1	245.0

30	South Lake	417.5	.054	5.7	10.6	411.8	406.9	283.6
32	Van Dyke	456.8	.066	6.9	12.8	449.9	444.0	286.7
33	Warren City	447.1	.063	5.1	9.4	442.0	437.7	336.2
34	Muskegon City	343.2	.052	5.1	9.5	338.1	333.7	300.4
35	Muskegon Heights	292.1	.055	6.3	9.0	385.8	283.1	266.0
37	Birmingham	445.0	.039	4.0	7.5	437.5	437.5	288.7
41	Clawson City #11	307.7	.045	5.7	10.7	302.0	297.0	247.4
43	Ferndale City	445.8	.055	6.3	11.6	439.5	434.2	267.9
44	Hazel Park City #8	348.3	.053	6.5	12.1	341.8	336.2	248.6
47	Lamphere #4 Fr.	332.2	.035	4.2	7.8	328.0	324.4	253.8
48	Madison Public	287.5	.040	5.3	9.9	282.2	277.6	240.3
49	Oak Park	466.3	.066	7.4	13.8	458.9	452.5	273.3
50	Pontiac	425.4	.065	6.6	12.3	418.8	413.1	292.8
52	Royal Oak	367.8	.047	5.5	10.3	362.3	357.5	259.6
53	Southfield Public	434.4	.050	5.2	9.7	429.2	424.7	287.5
54	Troy City	376.1	.055	6.5	12.2	369.6	363.9	257.1
57	Saginaw	339.3	.057	6.0	11.2	333.3	328.1	283.3
58	Ann Arbor City #1	502.4	.051	4.8	8.9	497.6	493.5	309.8
60	Ypsilanti City	391.5	.056	6.5	12.1	385.0	379.4	262.0
61	Allen Park	381.4	.052	7.0	13.0	374.4	368.4	262.3
63	Dearborn City	589.2	.065	5.0	9.2	584.2	580.0	345.3
64	Dearborn Twp. #8	271.7	.045	6.0	11.1	265.8	260.7	246.5

APPENDIX 3 continued

School District	(1) Total Operating Expenditures (per pupil) ($)	(2) Expenditures Income	(3) ΔE^a if $Ny^b = .7$ ($)	(4) ΔE if $Ny = 1.3$ ($)	(5) $E_1{}^c$ if $Ny = .7$ (1) − (3) ($)	(6) E_1 if $Ny = 1.3$ (1) − (4) ($)	(7) Mandated Expenditures Plus State Aid ($)
65 Detroit	415.7	.060	6.0	11.1	409.7	404.6	295.8
66 Ecorse Public	652.2	.124	7.2	13.4	645.0	638.8	383.0
67 Garden City	278.3	.045	6.0	11.1	272.3	267.2	229.1
68 Grosse Pointe	601.4	.047	4.3	7.9	597.1	593.5	315.8
69 Hamtramack	543.2	.075	5.6	10.4	537.6	532.8	377.3
71 Highland Park	603.7	.076	8.5	11.1	595.2	592.6	341.7
72 Inkster	359.9	.088	14.0	25.6	345.9	334.3	266.7
73 Lincoln Park	322.8	.050	7.0	13.1	315.8	309.7	256.7
74 Livonia	461.7	.059	6.5	12.0	455.2	449.7	276.7
75 Melvindale-North Allen Park	477.0	.072	9.0	16.6	468.0	450.4	272.5
78 River Rouge	601.0	.103	3.8	7.1	597.2	593.9	428.0
82 Trenton Public	400.5	.062	5.4	10.1	395.1	390.4	322.3
84 Wayne Comm.	385.7	.062	7.6	14.2	378.1	371.5	249.4
85 Wyandotte City	459.3	.069	7.5	13.9	451.8	445.4	278.6

a. ΔE = Estimated change in expenditures resulting from state aid.

b. Ny = Income elasticity of demand for education.

c. E_1 = Estimated initial expenditures.

APPENDIX 4
AN EMPIRICAL ANALYSIS
OF EDUCATIONAL EXPENDITURES

An estimation of some of the social and economic factors influencing per pupil operating expenditures on education was done as part of a preliminary empirical analysis. The method of estimation was a least squares multiple regression. The observations included the 52 Michigan school districts which could be reasonably well approximated by a combination of census tracts.[1]

The following social or economic factors were used to explain variations in per pupil operating expenditures: income per pupil, percentage of property classified as industrial, percentage of pupils attending nonpublic schools, and percentage of "recent migrants."

EXPECTED EFFECTS

Income

Income (I), defined in terms of family income per school child[2] plus state aid per pupil,[3] can be viewed as influencing both the demand for education and the ability of the district to finance educational expenditures. As noted earlier, the level of education of the parents is thought to be even more important than income in terms of their demand for education. Given the close correlation between income and education, however, income also serves as a proxy for the level of parental education. This reinforces the expected positive relationship between income and educational expenditures.

Industrial Property

The presence of industrial property (IP), defined as the percentage of the district's property classified as industrial,[4] also influences the resources available to the district. As long as district residents, as suppliers of labor or as consumers, do not pay the tax on industrial property (or conceive of themselves as paying it), the presence of industrial property lowers the "price" of education. Because of this, the presence of industrial property is expected to be associated with higher per pupil expenditures.

Nonpublic School Pupils and Recent Migrants

The present system of financing local district expenditures does not distinguish between groups of individuals who can be expected to have very different allegiances to the public schools. Ranking groups according to their expected allegiances (strong to weak) results in the following ordering:

(1) parents of public school children,
(2) parents of former (and future) public school children in this district,
(3) parents of former public school children not in this district and parents of future public school children who do not expect to be in this district, and
(4) parents of private school children.

The percentage of school children in nonpublic schools (NP)[5] is used as a proxy for the fourth group. This variable is expected to be negatively related to current operating expenditures. Recent migrants (RM), measured as the percentage of the district population five years or older which changed residence between 1950 and 1960,[6] is used as a proxy for group three. The assumption is that anyone who has moved within five years is more likely to have moved in the past or move in the future than one who has not moved recently. The recent migrant variable is also expected to be negatively related to current operating expenditures but less so than the percentage of nonpublic school children.

RESULTS

The estimation resulted in the following regression equation:

$$E/P = 142.3 + .04\ I + 3.1\ IP - 1.0\ NP - 2.2\ RM\ (R^2 = .66)$$
$$(.01)\quad (\ .4)\quad (1.1)\qquad (.9)$$

The net regression coefficients imply the following: on the average, a one dollar increase in the district's per pupil income is associated with a four cent increase in per pupil operating expenditures, all other things being equal; a one percent increase in the district's property classified as industrial is associated with a $3.10 increase in per pupil operating expenditures, and so forth.

Except for nonpublic school pupils, the net regression coefficients are consistent with the expectations indicated above. The income and industrial property variables are significant at the .01 level. The recent migrant variable is significant at the .02 level. The sign on the nonpublic school pupils variable is in the expected direction but the coefficient is less than its standard error.

It can be argued, however, that the 52 districts represent a population rather than a sample and that standard errors or measures of significance are meaningless, since they measure uncertainty with respect to the sampling variation.[7] In any case, the coefficient of partial determination (partial r^2)[8] indicates the relative importance of each of the variables. The partial r^2's for I, IP, NP, and RM are .71, .78, -.13, and -.33, respectively. It is clear that income and industrial property are both the most important explanatory variables and are of relatively equal importance. The percentage of recent migrants is moderately important and the percentage of nonpublic pupils is of little importance. The latter is contrary to expectation.

The R^2 of .66 indicates that these four explanatory variables account for 66% of the variation in per pupil operating expenditures. A more extensive list of social or economic factors would probably be required in order to account for more of the variation.

The net regression coefficients allow us to calculate elasticity coefficients. These are appropriately computed as the mean values of the variables. The income elasticity of demand for education is .73, implying that a 1% increase in income is a .73 increase in educational expenditures. The elasticity of per pupil expenditures with respect to the proportion of property which is industrial (and also the total property tax paid by industrial property) is .21. We can use this to approximate a price elasticity of demand for education. In this case, our interest is in the elasticity of per pupil expenditures with respect to a change in residential property tax (per family). This depends on $N_{IP} \times T_R/T_I$ where T_R = total residential tax and T_I = the amount of property taxes from industrial property. On the average, the relationship between residential property value and industrial property value is slightly more than 2.4 to 1 or in other words, residential property taxes are somewhat less than 2½ times industrial property tax collections. As a rough approximation, this implies a price elasticity of .51.

NOTES TO APPENDIX 4

1. U. S. Department of Commerce, Bureau of the Census (1960). The reason for the approximation is discussed in the text. See Notes to Chapter 5, footnote 16.

2. *Ibid.* Family income per school child is equal to

$$\frac{\text{median family income}}{\text{school enrollment per family}}$$

3. Michigan, State of [3]. Since state aid appears to be distributed in the form of a lump-sum grant for the 52 districts, then in terms of the partial equilibrium approach used in this study, state aid should be included in the district's income.

4. These percentages are estimates based on data for the muncipalities which overlie the districts. Michigan Municipal League (1963); and Detroit Metropolitan Area Regional Planning Commission (1959).

5. U. S. Department of Commerce, Bureau of the Census (1960).

6. *Ibid.*

7. Gensemer (1966): 33-36.

8. The partial r^2 of an independent variable X_1 measures the extent of variation explained by the introduction of X_1 holding the other variables in the equation constant.

BIBLIOGRAPHY

BARLOW, R. (1967) "Financing Public Schools in Michigan." Report to the Michigan School Finance Study (mimeo).

BAUMOL, W. J. (1965) Economic Theory and Operations Analysis. Englewood Cliffs, N.J.: Prentice-Hall.

BECKER, G. S. (1964) Human Capital. New York: National Bureau of Economic Research.

—— and B. CHISWICK (1966) "Education and the distribution of earnings." American Economic Review, Papers and Proceedings LVI (May): 358-369.

BENSON, C. S., ed. (1963) Perspectives on the Economics of Education. Boston: Houghton-Mifflin.

BISHOP, G. A. (1964) "Stimulative versus substitution effects of state school aid in New England." National Tax Journal XVII (June): 133-143.

BOWLES, S. and H. LEVIN (1968) "The determinants of scholastic achievement." The Journal of Human Resources III (Winter): 1-24.

BRAZER, H. E. (1961a) Taxation in Michigan: An Appraisal. Ann Arbor: Univ. of Michigan Institute of Public Administration.

—— (1961b) "The value of industrial property as a subject of taxation." Canadian Public Administration IV (June): 137-147.

—— (1959) "City Expenditures in the United States." Occasional Paper 66. New York: National Bureau of Economic Research.

BREAK, G. F. (1967) Intergovernmental Fiscal Relations in the United States. Washington, D.C.: Brookings Institution.

BUCHANAN, J. M. and M. E. KAFOLGIS (1963) "A note on public goods supply." American Economic Review LIII (June):

BURKE, A. J. (1957) Financing Public Schools in the United States. New York: Harper and Bros.

BURKHEAD, J. (1964) Public School Finance. Syracuse, N. Y.: Syracuse University Press.

—— and A. CAMPBELL (1968) "Public Policy in Urban America." In H. S. Perloff and L. Wingo, eds. Issues in Urban Economics. Baltimore: Johns Hopkins University Press.

BURKHEAD, J. with T. G. FOX and J. W. HOLLAND (1967) Input and Output in Large City High Schools. Syracuse, N.Y.: Syracuse University Press.

CAMPBELL, A., W. MILLER, P. CONVERSE and D. STOKES (1960) The American Voter. New York: John Wiley and Sons.

Citizens Research Council (1967) Comments. Detroit: Citizens Research Council of Michigan (April 3).

—— (1962) Comments. Detroit: Citizens Research Council of Michigan (March 17).

CLINE, D. C. and M. C. TAYLOR (1966) Michigan Tax Reform. East Lansing: Michigan State University.

COLEMAN, J. S. et al. (1966) Equality of Educational Opportunity. Washington, D.C.: Government Printing Office.

Detroit Metropolitan Area Regional Planning Commission (1959) 1958 Land Use in the Detroit Region. Detroit.

Economic Report of the President and Annual Report of the Council of Economic Advisers, 1964. Washington, D.C.: Government Printing Office.

FEIN, R. (1965) "Educational Patterns in Southern Migration." Reprint 104. Washington, D.C.: Brookings Institution.

GENSEMER, B. (1966) "Fiscal Policy Decisions of Local Governments in Urban Areas: Public Safety and Public Education." Ph.D. dissertation, The University of Michigan.

GREEN, C. and R. LAMPMAN (1967) "Schemes for transferring income to the poor." Industrial Relations VI (February): 121-137.

HANSEN, W. L. (1963) "Total and private rates of return on investments in schooling." Journal of Political Economy LXXI (April): 128-140.

HENDERSON, J. M. and R. E. QUANDT (1959) Microeconomic Theory. New York: McGraw-Hill.

HIRSCH, W. Z., E. W. SEGELHORST and M. J. MARCUS (1964) Spillover of Public Education Costs and Benefits. Los Angeles: University of California Institute for Government and Public Affairs.

JAMES, T., J. A. THOMAS and H. J. DYCK (1963) "Wealth, Expenditures and Decision-Making for Education." Unpublished report, Stanford University School of Education.

JOHNS, R. L. and E. L. MORPHIT (1963) "Developing the foundation program." Chapter 36 in C. S. Benson, ed. Perspective on the Economics of Education. Boston: Houghton-Mifflin.

LINDMAN, E. L. (1964) State School Support and Municipal Government Costs. Los Angeles: UCLA Press.

Manpower Report of the President and a Report on Manpower Requirements, Resources, Utilization and Training (1966) Washington, D.C.: Government Printing Office.

Michigan Educational Finance Study Commission (1956) "Report to the Governor." (mimeo, March 20) Lansing.

Michigan Municipal League (1963) Financial Abstracts. Ann Arbor.

Michigan, State of

[1] An analysis of the Revenues and Expenditures for 1964-65 (1966) Bulletin 1011, rev. Lansing: Board of Education.

[2] Annual Financial Report (Form B) for 1965-66. Lansing: Department of Education.

[3] Annual Statistical and Financial Reports for the Year 1961-62. Lansing: Department of Education.

[4a] Constitution (1908).

[4b] Constitution (1963).

[5] Budget Division. Detail of State Operations and Local Benefits Budgets for Fiscal Years 1960-1967.

[6] General School Laws (1960) Revision of 1959. Lansing: Speaker-Hines and Thomas.

[7] Legislative Service Bureau (1966) Supplement to the 1959 Revision of the General School Laws of Michigan As Enacted During the 1960, 1961, 1962, 1963, 1964, 1965, and 1966 Legislative Sessions. Lansing.

[8] News of the Week XXXI (February 21, 1964) Department of Public Instruction.

[9] Pittsfield Case of 1954. Michigan 388: 341.

[10] Public Acts, 1955.

[11] Public Acts, 1957.

[12] Public Acts, 1958.

[13] Public Acts, 1959.

[14] Public Acts, 1962.

[15] Public Acts, 1963.

[16] Public Acts, 1965.

[17] School Code of 1955.

[18] School Finance Study, Summary Report, 1967. Lansing: Department of Education.

MINER, J. (1963) Social and Economic Factors in Spending for Public Instruction. Syracuse, N. Y.: Syracuse University Press.

MORGAN, J., M. DAVID, W. COHEN and H. BRAZER (1962) Income and Welfare in the United States. New York: McGraw-Hill.

MORT, P. R., W. C. REUSSER and J. W. POLLEY (1960) Public School Finance: Its Background, Structure and Operation. New York: McGraw-Hill.

MUSGRAVE, R. A. (1959) The Theory of Public Finance. New York: McGraw-Hill.

and D. DAICOFF (1958) "Who pays the Michigan taxes?" in Michigan Tax Study, Staff Papers. Lansing.

RENSHAW, E. F. (1960) "A note on expenditure effects of state aid to education." Journal of Political Economy LXVIII (April): 170-174.

SACKS, S. and R. HARRIS (1964) "The determinants of state and local government expenditures and intergovernmental flows of funds." National Tax Journal XVII (March): 75-85.

SCHULTZ, T. (1961) "Education and economic growth" Social Forces Influencing American Education. Chicago: National Society for the Study of Education.

SLY, J., W. MILLER and J. A. ARNOLD (1953) Michigan State Aid Survey. Lansing.

STRAYER, G. D. and R. M. HAIG (1924) "The financing of education in the state of New York." Report of the Educational Finance Inquiry Commission. New York: Macmillan.

TABLEMAN, B. (1951) Paying for Public Schools in Michigan. Ann Arbor: University of Michigan Institute of Public Administration.

WEISBROD, B. A. (1964) External Benefits of Public Education: An Economic Analysis. Princeton: Princeton University Press.

WILLIAMS, A. (1963) Public Finance and Budgetary Policy. London: Allen and Unwin.

U. S. Bureau of the Budget (1966) The Budget of the United States

Government, Fiscal Year Ending June 30, 1967. Washington, D.C.: Government Printing Office.

U. S. Department of Commerce, Bureau of the Census (1960) U. S. Census of Population and Housing, 1960. Census Tracts. Washington, D.C.: Government Printing Office.